GLOBET

Travel

RIO DE JANEIRO

PAUL TINGAY

NEW
HOLLAND

NEW HOLLAND

First edition published in 2006
by New Holland Publishers (UK) Ltd
London • Cape Town • Sydney • Auckland
10 9 8 7 6 5 4 3 2 1

website: www.newhollandpublishers.com

Garfield House, 86 Edgware Road
London W2 2EA,
United Kingdom

80 McKenzie Street
Cape Town 8001,
South Africa

14 Aquatic Drive,
Frenchs Forest, NSW 2086,
Australia

218 Lake Road,
Northcote, Auckland,
New Zealand

Distributed in the USA by
The Globe Pequot Press, Connecticut

Keep us Current
Information in travel guides is apt to change, which is why
we regularly update our guides. We'd be grateful to receive
feedback if you've noted something we should include in
our updates. If you have new information, please share it
with us by writing to the Publishing Manager, Globetrotter,
at the office nearest to you (addresses on this page). The
most significant contribution to each new edition will
receive a free copy of the updated guide.

Publishing Manager (UK): Simon Pooley
Publishing Manager (SA): Thea Grobbelaar
DTP Cartographic Manager: Genené Hart
Editors: Alicha van Reenen, Melany McCallum
Design and DTP: Nicole Bannister
Cartographer: Genené Hart
Picture Researcher: Shavonne Johannes
Proofreader and Indexer: Claudia Dos Santos
Consultant: Alistair Campbell
Reproduction by Resolution, Cape Town.
Printed and bound by Times Offset (M) Sdn. Bhd., Malaysia.

Photographic Credits:
Tom Cockrem: pages 21, 22, 24, 33, 41, 48, 52, 55, 59,
69, 77, 81, 85, 86, 90, 109, 110; **jonarnold.com/Joe
Malone:** title page ; **BrazilPhotoBank/Rogerio Assis:** page
104; **BrazilPhotoBank/Katsuyoshi Tanaka:** cover;
BrazilPhotoBank/Mirian Fichtner: pages 92, 93, 107, 113;
BrazilPhotoBank/ Andre Teixeira/AG: page 108;
BrazilPhotoBank/Jorge William/AG: page 96;
BrazilPhotoBank/Adriana Zehbrauskas: page 100;
BrazilPhotoBank/Márcia Zoet/Illumina: page 19, 91;
Brazil Photo/Ricardo Funari: pages 6, 40, 44, 49, 75, 84,
94, 99, 101; **Larry Luxner:** pages 15, 20; **Buddy Mays:**
page 68; **photographersdirect.com/Ana Branco/
Argosfoto:** page 78; **photographersdirect.com/
Jahanimage:** page 54; **photographersdirect.com/Picture
Hunting World:** page 4; **photographersdirect.com/
Douglas Pulsipher:** page 56; **Pictures Colour Library:**
pages 7, 50; **Brian Richards:** pages 42, 83; **Paul Tingay:**
pages 8, 9, 11, 12, 13, 14, 16, 18, 23, 26, 27, 29, 34, 35,
36, 37, 38, 46, 47, 60, 62, 64, 67, 70, 71, 82, 88, 98;
World Picture News/Douglas Harrison Engle: page 102;
World Picture News/Paulo Fridman: pages 25, 30, 72,
111; **World Picture News/Casey Kelbaugh:** page 61.

Acknowledgements
The publishers and author would like to thank Paula
Medeiros, Peter Fry and above all Raphael Yuri Shamoon
Braga, the author's constant and companionable guide in
the marvellous city.

Cover: *Cable car up to Sugar Loaf Mountain.*
Title page: *Surf, palms and Pablo Picasso's wavy paving.*

CONTENTS

1
Introducing
Rio de Janeiro

Gonçalho Coelho and his sea captains, Gaspar de Lemos and André Gonçalves, must have reflected as did Luis Vaz de Camões in his epic Lusiads poem: 'Our heavy anchors to the waves were cast. But where are we, in what unchartered world?' They were, in fact, in **Guanabara Bay**. Thinking it a river, they named it the River of January. The date was 1 January 1502, and **Rio de Janeiro** had been discovered by Europeans for the first time.

Rio is an unbelievably vibrant city of 12 million people, spread out along and between 60km (37 miles) of beaches and forested mountains. It is the people that make Rio, the descendants of the exotic mix during the course of 500 years of Portuguese colonists, African slaves, indigenous Indians and waves of immigrants from Europe and even Japan. Together these Cariocas have given us samba, sensuality, football and, of course, *Carnaval*, the greatest extravaganza on earth.

THE LAND

Rio de Janeiro is a city of the sea and playground of the world. The blue **Atlantic** surrounds and infiltrates its sinuous bays, beaches and inlets for 30km (20 miles) north and south of downtown **Centro**, and stretches another 20km (12.5 miles) of crowded urban conurbation inland. It is a city of rugged forested mountains that creep down to the very edge of every *bairro* (neighbourhood), highway and alluvial beach promenade. The pristine Brazilwood rainforest and wetlands of the

TOP ATTRACTIONS

*** **Carnaval:** samba, sequins, floats, feathers and the body beautiful.
*** **Copacabana and Ipanema beaches:** scimitars of sand, surf, mosaic promenades and people-watching.
*** **Sugar Loaf (Pão de Açúcar):** cable car to a glittering sunset panorama of Rio.
*** **Christ the Redeemer statue:** forest train ride up 710m (2943ft) Corcovado Peak. 360º postcard.
** **Sidewalk cafés:** *chopp* draught beer, *pasteis*, prawns and gossip.

Opposite: *Christ the Redeemer statue towers over all of Rio.*

Opposite: *Copacabana. Beach of dreams.*
Below: *Dawn worshippers on Ipanema beach.*

early colonists have all but gone, replaced during 500 years by reclaimed land, skyscrapers, mountain tunnels, ever-expanding suburbs, a metro, beach hotels, parks, old-world squares of trees and cafés, legions of condominiums, and thundering traffic. There are, however, still lovely lagoons near the botanical gardens and inland from the 20km (12.5-mile) **Barra Beach**. Right in the middle of it all is **Tijuca**, the largest urban forest in the world. In a helicopter (a favourite excursion) or from **Corcovado Peak**, you can just see the **Serra do Mar** mountains that flank the city and offer within its cool valleys, delightful day trips to such old colonial towns as **Petrópolis**, the summer retreat of the Portuguese royal court (*see* page 16) 200 years ago.

The city is divided into three *zonas*: the industrial **Zona Norte** (and international airport), **Zona Sul**, in the south, with the business **Centro** in the middle. Through the centuries (particularly when faster electric trams replaced the donkey-drawn variety) the neighbourhoods of colonial days were superseded in popularity by such brash new southern suburbs as Copacabana in the 1930s; then **Leblon** and finally, with super highways tunnelling through the mountains, the condominiums of the wealthy at **Barra**.

Zona Norte

Taking the outstretched arms of the **Redeemer** atop **Corcovado Peak** as the midpoint, the north starts at the Central Metro Station near the **Quinta da Boa Vista Park** and **National Museum,** and stretches in a vast polyglot of suburbs and industrial sites past the international airport. This was a natural expansion as the *baixadas* (lowlands) were obviously less mountainous and thus much more

accessible than near the famous southern beach resorts. The north is not particularly attractive, but if you are interested in ordinary folk, this is where their daily hard work and lives are concentrated. It has the advantage of having markets that are far cheaper than in the leafy suburbs of Ipanema and Leblon in the south. Cariocas, as people born in Rio de Janeiro call themselves,

seldom stare or bother visitors. Even less so here. They are too busy trying to survive.

The north can lay claim to the famous **Maracanã** (green parrot) **Football Stadium**, the emperor's old residence in the **Quinta da Boa Vista** and above all the **Sambódromo**, where **Carnaval** now mainly takes place. When it opened in 1810, the **English Cemetery** in the Rua da Gambôa was the only Church of England cemetery allowed. The small English community was forbidden to bury their dead in the church itself, hence the cemetery.

Centro

Castelo (Castle Hill) with its fort was Rio's most notable landmark in the early 16th century. It faced **Guanabara Bay**, the fertile sea as the original Indians knew it, and dates from 1567 when **Estácio de Sá**, the son of Brazil's Governor, finally defeated the French colonists who had the nerve to intrude into Portugal's empire. The hill and fort have long since been raised and replaced by **Av Presidente Antônio Carlos,** as there was a danger of landslides to the growing city. The only remaining remnant is a tiny cobbled street known as **Ladeira da Misericordia**. It looks a little forlorn too.

Central Rio is not only the business heart of town but also the oldest part, with a wealth of historical buildings to feast on. It stretches from the sea and **Santos Dumont Domestic Airport**, inland through **Imperial Square** (or **Praça 15 de Novembro**), as far as the little *bondinho* train that clatters up to the old Bohemian

NUMBERS GAME

Standing at a bus stop in Rio you might see a scruffy list of numbers pinned to a tree. These are the lucky winners of that day's *jogo do bicho* or numbers game. Turn around and you might see an innocuous gent sitting at a small table on the street, taking the bets. It's all 100% illegal and controlled by crime bosses in the *favelas* (see page 9) who even used to get themselves elected as presidents of samba schools in return for financial backing.

CARNAVAL

• March 1786: the first Parade in Rio.
• Estácio suburb: the first samba school opens in 1928.
• Flag bearer or *porta bandeira*: the important woman who leads each samba school in the procession. If she has superb style, she wins many points for her school.
• Samba schools rehearse for six months prior to Carnaval.
• There are still plenty of the original street Carnavals left.

THE AMAZON

The Amazon Jungle is the world's largest tropical rain-forest, cut through by the Amazon River, the world's largest but only second longest. The Nile beats it by 179km (111 miles). With its 1100 tributaries it produces an incredible 20% of the world's fresh water.

NIGHTLIFE

• There are no limits to drinking hours in Rio.
• You will be handed a card as you enter a nightclub. Your drinks are ticked off against it.
• For a Saturday or Tuesday night street party: Salgueiro Samba School in rehearsal.
• Carioca Da Gema. Live samba and chorinho music. Rua Mem de Sá, 79. Lapa.
• Casa Rosa – Samba Da Alice. Music and singsongs. Rua Alice 550, Laranjeiras.
• Bar foods can include *torreso* or grilled pork rinds, deep-fried *aipim frito* (cassava) and *Porção de pasteis*, (tiny Cornish pasties filled with shrim**ps).**

hilltop suburb of **Santa Teresa** on one side, and **Campo de Santana Park** and Rio's railway station on the other. **Av Presidente Vargas**, which is 4.5km (3 miles) long and 90m (300ft) wide, stretches to the north, while the 2km (1.2-mile) **Av Rio Branco** slices through the middle.

Over a span of 400 years, at least 30 historic churches have been built in Centro (a new one is the Aztec pyramid-shaped **Catedral Metropolitana**). Particularly worth visiting are the **Convento and Igreja de Santo Antônio** in Largo da Carioca Square and **Mosteiro de São Bento** (St Benedict's Monastery), dating back to the 16th century, the oldest in the city. It sits on top of a hill near Praça Mauá on the bay.

Rio is larger than Sydney, Johannesburg, or London, and it is densely populated. Expect to find downtown skyscrapers, flyovers, banks, commuters and traffic, especially cavalry charges of buses. It is rich in history and layered with centuries of architectural development. There is no shortage of fountains, statues, leafy boule-vards and pavement cafés, as well as dozens of superb museums and historical sites, some dating back before Cape Town or New York were settled by Europeans.

Start your walkabout at Praça 15 de Novembro, or as it is more commonly called, *Praça Quinze*.

Zona Sul

Zona Sul stretches from **Flamengo** past **Sugar Loaf** through to **Copacabana**, **Ipanema**, **Gávea** and the whole coastal stretch almost up to **Barra da Tijuca**. It incorporates the great mountain ranges of southern **Tijuca**, the *Redentor* on **Corcovado** and smart suburbs such as **Cosme Velho**, **Leblon** and **Jardim Botânico**, as well as **Lagoa Rodrigo de Freitas**, Rio's weekend water-sports retreat. The heart of the south is probably anywhere you see one of the ubiquitous Zona Sul supermarkets. **Copacabana**'s sands, the glitzy fashion shops of **Ipanema** and the clubs of **Lagoa** and the elegant streets of **Urca**, make Zona Sul the preferred residential area.

Ipanema and Copacabana are the quintessential sea and sun kingdoms. Here one comes to jog, sip iced coconut juice on the promenades and watch the girls play volleyball.

Barra da Tijuca, the Miami condominium coast of Rio, is a Sunday favourite for surfing, tanning and family barbeques, while its vast shopping malls try to out-USA each other.

The south is a good address especially if you can afford Gávea, Leblon or São Conrado. It is, however, not all almond-tree avenues, palm-swept beaches, bossa nova and regattas on the lagoon. With the exception of upper-crust Urca around Sugar Loaf with its plastic surgeons and military officers' villas, Zona Sul is a frenetic mix of boutique businesses, tourism hotels, surfers, sidewalk corn-on-the-cob vendors and Rio's usual avalanche of Marco Polo buses hurtling through mountain-piercing tunnels.

Favelas

In the last 200 years, cities all over the world have had to face sudden mass influx. It led to the gin palaces of London, the mobsters of Chicago, overcrowding, malnutrition, infant mortality, crime, numbing poverty and lack of housing. For the poor people of Rio it has been no different.

Rio is basically a first-world city, so naturally Cariocas are concerned, at times even embarrassed, by the hillsides of poverty – some would call them slums – that are visible in Rio. There is great compassion, but no one has a magic remedy. At least there is the will, technical expertise and the prospect of a vibrant economy. Brazil is a rich country with the comfort of knowing that many who are doing well today are the children of parents who once lived in the *favelas*. It will, however, take many years before all in Rio win

MUST DO

• **Santa Teresa:** picturesque old cobbled hilltop village reached by a tiny toy-town train, the *bondinho*.
• **Copacabana:** fort and military museum.
• An *acai-guaraná* 'shake' (with granola sprinkling): on Ipanema Beach from one of the kiosks.
• **Jardim Botânico** (Botanical Gardens): avenues of imperial palms and green-graced solitude.
• **Ipanema shopping:** everything a deep pocket could desire; Italian restaurants.
• **Breakfast at Copacabana Palace:** 1930s elegance; will cost you a fortune but the staff speak perfect 'American'.

Opposite: *Rio Centro, the heart of the city.*
Below: *A Santa Teresa artist issues a warning.*

• The word *favela* comes from the Portuguese word for nettles.
• The *favelas* twinkle at night, mainly from electricity the inhabitants have stolen by tapping into power lines.
• *Favelas* are usually on hills surrounded by wealthier areas.
• The several storey high houses are nearly all self-made of breezeblocks – they are not tin and plastic shanties.
• The seat on the back of a motorbike taxi is the way to get up the steep rough streets.
• Cocaine and crime (the gangsters are young, armed and ruthless) are features of the *favela*. Each *favela* usually has a *boca* (mouth), where drugs are sold.
• *Favela* folk are generally hard-working ordinary people.
• *Favela* dwellers are no longer forced to move. They have become accepted as part of the city.

O Globo, Rio's largest daily, publishes a half-page summary of Rio State and all Brazil's weather. Colourful graphics cover temperature, times of sunrise and sunset, moon phases, rainfall, and even those Rio beaches that may, that week, be subject to pollution (*própria* or *imprópria*). Plus minimum and maximum temperatures in major world cities from *São Francisco* to *Londres* to *Jerusalém*.

the affluent lifestyle of such western cities as Berlin, Melbourne or Tokyo. One thing is certain: the poor people of Rio are not ignored. The elderly blind lady sitting at the pavement corner of a restaurant who is given a *cafezinho* by a waiter, the wheelchair-bound man who is helped to sell combs and matches (and allowed to sleep on the street where he runs his business), the children who hand out flyers, the shoeshine man who is adopted by a kiosk owner on Copa Promenade – the folk of Rio seem to have the same philosophy as the followers of Islam and Hinduism, that the poor are a blessing from God. This, however, is not enough. The authorities will need to hold a very tough vision before them if they are to short-circuit the awful experiences of other great cities.

Climate

Rio de Janeiro lies on the Atlantic coast in the tropics, but is sufficiently south of the equator, right on Capricorn, to have cool winter nights in the dry season (June–August). Otherwise it is hot, rainy and often humid, with temperatures sometimes exceeding 30ºC (80ºF), particularly between December and March, but often with light refreshing winds. Shorts, T-shirts, slip-slops, hat and umbrella are the order of the day.

HISTORY IN BRIEF

Man, we believe, first emerged from the forests of East Africa some two million years ago. With the passing of time, he migrated to the Middle East, Europe, India, China, the Siberian wastes and across the then land-bridge of the Bering Strait into North America and

RIO DE JANEIRO	J	F	M	A	M	J	J	A	S	O	N	D
AV MAX TEMP. ºC	29	29	28	27	25	24	24	24	24	25	26	28
AV MIN TEMP. ºC	23	23	22	21	19	18	17	18	18	19	20	22
AV MAX TEMP. ºF	84	85	83	80	77	76	75	76	75	77	79	82
AV MIN TEMP. ºF	73	73	72	69	66	64	63	64	65	66	68	71
HOURS OF SUN DAILY	7	7	7	6	6	6	6	7	5	5	6	6
RAINFALL mm	122	114	122	102	79	53	51	51	56	81	96	132
RAINFALL in.	4.8	4.5	4.8	4	3.1	2.1	2	2	2.2	3.2	3.8	5.2
DAYS OF RAINFALL	13	11	12	10	10	7	7	7	11	13	13	14

eventually down into South America. Thus man was probably originally in Brazil some 50,000 years ago. Archaeological research and rock paintings tell us that hunter-gatherers in the days before settled agriculture, lived along the **Amazon**, 700km (440 miles) upriver, 12,000 years ago. But it was not until 2000 years ago that a more settled albeit slash-and-burn cultivation of cereal crops began. Manioc and West Indies' maize – those great South American staples – are now grown all over the world.

Above: *A huge, romanticized mural in Copacabana Fort Museum of the first meeting between Portuguese navigators and Brazilian Indians.*

Small groups of people who came to be called **Indians**, because the Portuguese and the Spanish initially thought they had arrived on the east coast of India, lived in and around Rio about 5000 years ago. Archaeologists have deduced this from excavating coastal burial, cooking and dwelling sites known as *sambaquis*, which left mounds of seafood shells, the odd arrowhead and, perhaps, a necklace for modern man to ponder over.

When the **Portuguese** arrived at the turn of the 15th century there were probably about 1000 different **Indian** clans in Brazil, some 2–6 million people – a vague guesstimate, as tropical forests hide a lot and don't make for scientific accuracy. They lived in sophisticated communal huts, but moved regularly. All were expert at hunting, pottery and war. Like the modern Cariocas, music, games and dancing were favourite pastimes. They had no iron tools or the wheel. The people in the Rio area referred to themselves as **Tupi**, the language they spoke.

Men of the Sea

Religion has always generated prodigious energy: Christian evangelism during the Roman Empire, the Arab-Islamic conquest of the Middle East and North Africa, the Crusades. It was possibly the main impetus for the great Portuguese discoveries during the 15th and

CARIOCA

In 1503–04 **Gonçalo Coelho**, one of the few Portuguese settlers in the new River of January, built himself a house that he chiselled from stone and mud bricks on the long sweep of beach we now call Flamengo (at the time, Praia de Uruçumirim). Watching, fascinated, were a group of Tomoio Indians. They had never seen iron tools before, let alone a house of anything but palm thatch. And so they named Coelho and his colleagues 'Carioca', with 'cari' meaning white and 'oca' meaning stones – 'the people of the white stone houses'. The *O Globo* newspaper today has a regular cartoon called Cariocaturas.

Above: *Painting by Camões of Copacabana, Ipanema and the church where Fort Copacabana now stands.*

16th centuries. After all, what nobler inspiration could one have to venture into the unknown – apart from gold, ivory and the fabulous spices of the East – than to convert the heathen to what the Portuguese and Spanish often named their settlements: Santa Cruz, the Holy Cross.

European Christianity, already in the turmoil and decay that would lead to the Protestant Reformation, was going through a period of fundamentalism not unlike Islam today. And it was to broach Islam's grip on the Mediterranean and Middle East that the Portuguese

HISTORICAL CALENDAR

50,000BC Hunter-gatherers first arrive in Brazil from North America.

3000BC Semi-nomadic communities of 'Indians', particularly the Tupi-Guarani linguistic family, live along the Atlantic coast.

1000AD Norwegian Leif Ericson is driven onto the North American coast which he calls Vinland after the wild grapes his sailors find there.

12 Oct 1492 Genoese adventurer Cristoforo Colombo sets anchor in the Bahamas, naming it San Salvador.

21 Apr 1500 Portuguese Commander Pedro Cabral, sailing to India from the Cape Verde Islands, lands in Brazil, which he names Terra da Vera Cruz (Land of the True Cross).

1501–02 Florentine navigator Amerigo Vespucci sails the length of this landmass to a point 32° S.L. and thinks he

has found a 'new world'.

01 Jan 1502 Gonçalho Çoelho discovers and names Rio, the River of January.

1507 German geographer, Martin Waldseemüller, suggests this new world be called America, a name that initially only applied to South America.

1567 'City' of Rio de Janeiro is established on today's site.

1660 Rio's population: some 5000 souls, mainly Indian.

1700s Rio now a major port for exporting sugar and gold.

1550–1888 3.5 million slaves are imported into Brazil, mainly from Africa.

1763 Rio (pop 50,000) declared the capital of Brazil.

1807 The Portuguese royal court under King João VI moves to Brazil to escape Napoleon in Europe.

1822 Dom Pedro I declares he will not go back to

Portugal, declares Brazil independent of the motherland and himself emperor.

1800s Coffee boom in Brazil.

1889–1930 The first Republic. During this period 4M immigrants came to Brazil.

1939–45 Brazil is the only South American state to take part in WWII. And on the side of the democracies.

20th century 'Economic Miracle'. Industrial production increased by 80%.

1960 Brasilia takes over from Rio as the nation's capital.

1961 President Goulart tries to ban Rio's bikinis and gets burnt in the process.

1964–84 Military dictatorship. Some of the best samba groups emerge to ridicule the military regimes.

2002 Lula becomes the 'Peoples' President'. He demands a seat for Brazil on the UN Security Council.

sought another route to India. As early as the 13th century, Portuguese ships had begun inching down the west coast of Africa, a process that accelerated with the accession to the throne of **Prince Henry the Navigator** (1394–1460), patron of discovery and science. In 1487 **Bartholomeu Dias** rounded the Cape of Good Hope. In 1492 the Italian, **Cristoforo Colombo**, in the service of Spain, reached the West Indies and Cuba, and six years later Portuguese **Admiral Vasco da Gama** reached India.

Eight years on, in 1500, **Pedro Álvares Cabral**, with 13 ships and 1200 crew, set sail for Kolkata, was blown off course in the Atlantic (so historians believe) and landed at today's **Porto Seguro**, Bahia, on 22 April 1500. Here, 1000km (620 miles) north of Rio, they built a stone *padrão* cross, to signify that this new land, which they called **Terra da Vera Cruz**, belonged to Portugal. They were not terribly taken with the rather daunting Brazilian forests and their *pão brasil*, Brazilian dyewood trees, let alone settling. They did, however, persuade the curious Indians they met to kneel to the cross. And then as the poet Fernando Pessoa wrote, 'Mighty is the labour, small the human source, I, … Navigator, abandoned this cross upon the golden strand and set another course.'

Guanabara Bay

A few ships periodically collected Brazilwood, which was used for red dye, but it was not until 1555 when a French expedition landed settlers on an island in Guanabara Bay to exploit the same Brazilwood near Cabo Frio, that the Portuguese remembered they had been there first. They attacked and defeated the French and their Tamoio Indian allies. The French, however, would not go away, so **Estácio de Sá**, nephew of Brazil's Portuguese governor took control. He started by erecting a rather scruffy settlement

---

MIGRATION

There is no such phenomenon as an 'indigenous' people, although we often refer to those who we believe were first in a particular country, such as the San of Africa, the Celts of Europe or the Indians of Brazil, as indigenous. All nations, all tribes, all people were immigrants before they became indigenous. Except perhaps Adam and Eve.

TREASURE TROVE

Brazil's stones include:
• **aquamarine**: the colour of coral seas.
• **amethyst**: deep purple beauty.
• **diamond**: love forever.
• **emerald**: green; gorgeous.
• **imperial topaz**: claret stone of Egyptian sun god, Ra.

Below: *Sunrise over the Guanabara hills and Copa Bay.*

• **Phoenicia:** a maritime
nation 3000 years ago,
where Lebanon, Syria and
Israel are today; believed to
have sailed around Africa's
Cape of Good Hope.
• **China:** Chinese junks (the
word is of Javanese origin)
reached East Africa long
before the Portuguese.
• **Indonesia:** Millennia ago,
Indonesian voyagers settled
in Madagascar, probably
sailing via India.
• **Scandanavia:** the Norse-
man Leif Ericsson landed in
America in AD1000, found
grapes growing and called
it Vinland.
• **Spain:** Fernão de
Magalhães, he of the
Magellan Strait at the tip
of South America, circum-
navigated the globe
(1519–1522).

Below: *Old Rio. Ipanema
Beach leading off Rodrigo
de Freitas Lagoon. Paint-
ing by Camões, 1870.*

of palm leaves surrounded by a palisade on the **Praia
de Fora** outer beach, a promontory below and to the
north of today's Sugar Loaf Mountain. The French
returned and were again subdued, enabling the 'city' to
be moved in 1567 to the more easily defended **Morro
de São Januário** (now called **Morro do Castelo**) further
around Guanabara Bay and near today's **Centro**. The
old settlement, or **Vila Velho**, below Sugar Loaf would
eventually become a part of **Urca** which through the
centuries has always remained a military area, being
strategically placed at the entrance to Guanabara Bay.
In the 17th century the sturdy **St John's Fortress** was
constructed and no more was heard of the French.

Mud, Mangroves and Malaria

In spite of the heat, disease and constant attacks by the
indigenous Indians, who by now had the measure of
these interlopers from the sea, the newly fortified town,
renamed **São Sebastião do Rio de Janeiro** managed to
hold out and expand. The initial population was some
500 souls who lost no time in trying to enslave the locals
to cut Brazilwood trees (from *brasa* – glowing coals of
the red wood) for export, and later to plant sugar cane,
discovered in the West Indies by the first conquistadors
and initially used in Europe as a medicine. Fortunately
the colonists soon realized the value of such local crops
as manioc, potatoes, tomatoes and tobacco, as well as
fish from Guanabara Bay. By the end of the 16th century, the Dutch in particular had begun to attack the
Portuguese empire and Portugal was not free of
European aggression and Spanish rivalry
until 1654. English King Charles II's marriage to Catherine, daughter of John IV
of Portugal, further strengthened the
mother country's hold on Brazil. Rio
expanded along the waterfront north
from Praça 15 and by 1660 the population had reached 5000, mostly Indian.

The story of the Indians of Brazil is
not a happy one. Initially the Indians

welcomed the Portuguese and traded with them. But possibly as a result of Portugal's centuries-long conflict with the Moors or African Arabs, the Portuguese came to distrust and denigrate all non-Christian foreigners. However, labour was vital for the new sugar plantations, so Indians were hunted down and enslaved.

Above: *Our little granules of sugar start their life in metres-high sticks of cane, often chewed raw.*

The cultural, economic and religious life of Rio received a considerable boost with the arrival of the Christian Orders, Benedictines, Franciscans, and Jesuits. Gold began to flow from the Minas Gerais interior, tempting the Dutch once again to attack between 1710 and 1711. The French, hot on their heels, even captured the city in 1711, sacked it and only handed it back when the citizenry paid a hefty ransom in gold, sugar and cattle. By now, sugar exports had made Rio the third largest city in Brazil after Recife and Salvador.

Swing Low, Sweet Chariot

African slaves from Ghana and Angola started to arrive in Brazil by 1550. The harsh logic was that they were less susceptible to both European and tropical diseases and prepared to work harder than the hunter-gatherer Indians on the sugar-cane plantations and mills that began to proliferate around the mouths of rivers, where there were rich soils and navigable bays such as Rio de Janeiro. Up to 150 slaves were employed on each plantation and some 3.5 million slaves were imported into Brazil from 1550 until slavery was abolished in 1888. Slaves worked up to 17 hours a day, disease (of which malaria and dysentery were but two) was a killer in the awful conditions, they were not allowed family life (children of slaves belonged to the master) and Africans from the same tribal area were split up to avoid

SUGAR-SWEET

There are sugar birds, sugar bushes, sugar loaves and sugar daddies. Cane sugar was one of the great discoveries of the new world of the Americas. The Brazilian colonial government welcomed the Jesuits (the Society of Jesus, formed by Ignatius of Loyola in 1534) but expected them to support themselves. To that end in about 1583 the Fathers built three sugar mills and plantations on a vast tract of land that today includes Tijuca suburb, Maracanã Stadium, Quinta da Boa Vista and São Cristóvão all the way to Guanabara Bay, but lost them when they were expelled from Brazil in 1759.

Above: *Equestrian statue of General Manuel Luiz Osório who led Brazil's army in the 1864–70 war with Paraguay.*

collective revolt. Islamic slaves were particularly feared. However, some slaves working on the gold fields were given a percentage of what they found and managed to buy their freedom.

By 1750 the gold rush was over. Former miners, desperate for work, poured into Rio which as a result of the gold trade became Brazil's capital in 1763. The population at the time had grown to 50,000 and the city experienced a boom. Fortifications were extended, churches built, streets paved and a canal built to bring the Carioca River to the public fountains in the square of the same name. The new Praça 15 Square was opened and major new public works inaugurated. The city expanded in all directions. A new confident Brazil tried to free itself of the mother country in 1789. But the revolt leader, **Joaquim José da Silva Xavier**, nicknamed the tooth-puller or Tiradentes, was betrayed and horribly executed.

Empire and Republic

In 1807, **Napoleon**, the French military genius and dictator, was about to invade Portugal. To avoid conflict, Portugal's Prince Regent (later King João VI), protected by a British naval escort, hurriedly evacuated Lisbon and moved the whole royal court to Rio. Forty ships and 15,000 people. The downside for the Cariocas was that many had to move as rents soared, the best homes going to the king's wealthy entourage.

The king soon established the Bank of Brazil, Law Courts, School of Medicine, Naval Academy and his pet project, Jardim Botânico, plus a palace at Quinta da Boa Vista. By 1821, however, he was forced to return to Portugal where revolt was seething, leaving his son **Pedro** as Prince Regent. Born Brazilians didn't like the idea of having to drop their exalted partnership with royalty and return to colonial status. So between them and Pedro, who took his father's admonition to 'take hold of the kingdom' to heart, they declared 'Independence or Death'. On 1 December 1822, Pedro, emulating

Napoleon, went further and had himself crowned Emperor of Brazil. All of which the demoralized Portugal, facing revolt at home and aggressive competition from the British abroad in the Brazilian trade, meekly accepted. Dom Pedro I didn't last long. After nine years he was forced to resign in favour of his five-year-old son, Pedro de Alacantara, who became **Pedro II**. In 1834, Rio was declared the capital of the Brazilian empire over which the new emperor ruled very successfully from 1840–89. Coffee, industry, railroad construction, stock raising and sugar all flourished. European immigration developed into a flood. The emperor unfortunately allowed his generals to control foreign policy which led to war with Paraguay, the bloodiest in South America's history. In 1850 Brazil had a population of 8 million of whom 2.5 million were slaves.

The end of slavery also marked the end of empire with a bloodless coup orchestrated by **General Manoel Deodoro da Fonseca** who occupied Rio de Janeiro on 15 November 1889. The late 19th and early 20th centuries were marked by dictatorship, agricultural expansion, particularly coffee, social unrest and the Great Depression of 1928. Immigration led to increased mining, cattle ranching on the *fazendas*, trade and forestry. Rubber or *Hevea Brasiliensis* revolutionized the pneumatic tyre.

Rio's narrow and picturesque streets were driven right through during 1904 and 1905 with the new 33m (110ft) wide Avenida Central, later renamed **Avenida Rio Branco**. The Morro do Castelo was levelled in the 1920s, the earth being used for **Santos Dumont Airport**.

Modern Times

Brazil was the only South American state to play an active part in World War II. Five thousand soldiers fought in Italy against Hitler. The Communist party was outlawed in 1947 and in 1950 the popular **Getúlio Vargas**

SLAVERY

- Prince Henry the Navigator tried hard to eradicate slavery that had begun with the Portuguese exploration of Africa.
- Haitian slaves revolted and in 1804 became the first independent colony of our era.
- UK: first nation in modern times to abolish slavery (1807).
- Liberia was founded in 1822 as a colony for freed slaves.
- American Civil War (1861–65) was partly over the issue of abolition of slavery.
- David Livingstone did much to expose slavery in Africa.
- Brazilian slaves revolted and fled to the bush to form communities called *quilombos*.
- Lawyer Joaquim Nabuco led Brazilian abolition movement which ended slavery (1888).
- Saudia Arabia abolished slavery in 1962.
- Slavery is still rampant in parts of Sahelian and Sudanese Africa.
- Child trafficking and religious subjugation of women are modern forms of slavery.

Below: *Watch World Cup Football to see victorious waves of the Brazilian flag.*

was re-elected president, only to dramatically shoot himself on 24 August 1954 in the **Catete Palace** following a scandal and pressure from the military to resign.

Jucelino Kubitschek or 'JK', the next president, promised '50 years of economic development in five'. And, true enough, the next decade saw 'the economic miracle'. Industrial production increased by 80% and, unfortunately for Rio, the building of **Brasilia** as the new capital 1145km (715 miles) inland. But Brazil had still not lost its penchant for autocratic government. **President Janio Quadros** even tried to ban Rio's bikinis in 1961. **João 'Jango' Goulart** was deposed by the generals in 1964, and for the next 20 years these military boys from Brazil, who were often opposed by the Cariocas of Rio, clamped down on free speech, outlawed political parties and, particularly in the late 1960s, tortured and assassinated those they didn't like. In 1985 **Tancredo Neves**, to the surprise of the military, was enthusiastically elected president, but died before he could assume office.

Meanwhile, in the *favelas,* on the mines, and in particular in the burgeoning automobile industry, a new working-class movement was rapidly gaining momentum, led by dynamic trade unionist **Luíz Inácio da Silva**, or simply Lula, who had his eye on the presidency. He narrowly lost to **Fernando Collor de Mello** in 1989 and to **Fernando Henrique Cardoso** in 1994 and 1998 but in 2002 he became the 'Peoples' President' of Brazil.

GOVERNMENT AND ECONOMY

Brazil is the only truly federal nation in South America, perhaps because it is infinitely larger than its neighbours, (it occupies half the continent) and borders all but two of them. Four out of five Brazilians live in cities, mainly along the Atlantic coast. Rio City is part of Rio State, which in turn is one of the 28 states of the **República Federativa do Brasil**, governed by an executive president and bicameral legislature consisting of a Senate and Chamber of Deputies. Everyone over 16 can vote.

The **Palácio Guanabara** in Laranjeiras in Rio is where Rio's State Government is centred, while Legislative Assembly debates take place in the **Palácio Tiradentes** in Centro. Every municipality or *prefeitura* has a popularly elected mayor and a local council. The mayor's parlour is in the Palácio da Cidade in Botafogo.

Rio is to some extent a world apart from the rest of Brazil. But fun, frivolity and fabulous beaches do not altogether go with the serious business of Brazil's new Peoples' President **Luís Inácio (Lula) da Silva** who has promised to bring *mudança* (change): zero hunger, tax reduction, literacy within three years, 10 million jobs, inflation vanquished and serious reform of the *morisade* judiciary – for Lula and Brazil a huge credibility shock of ambitious programmes while of course still trying to retain the goodwill of foreign investors and the IMF. Rio de Janeiro state is Brazil's second largest industrial base, with steel, mining, and military industries. Rio has a plethora of universities and renowned beauty enhancing plastic surgery clinics; it is also a major media nexus (*Globo*) and its *novellas* (TV soaps) are exported worldwide. The city is home to 40% of Brazil's software development.

Above: *Steel, automobiles and heavy industry. Brazil's industrial output is booming.*
Opposite: *Brazil's currency notes. There is a R$100 note and even a plastic R$10 note.*

Developing Giant

São Paulo (pronounced *Sow Powloo*) is the necessary but grim powerhouse of Brazil. Not a great deal of love is lost between Cariocas and Paulistas, if only reflected on the football field. The Brazilian economy, the world's ninth largest with a workforce of 75 million, expanded by 5% in 2004. Brazil is the world's largest producer of coffee, the largest exporter of sugar and orange juice, the second largest exporter of soya and the third largest of beef and chicken. Rio is the centre of Brazil's oil industry, the oil wells of the Campos Basin being offshore. Some 70% of the nation's production of oil, pumped by Petrobrás, Texaco and Shell, is channelled through Rio. There are two nuclear energy power plants not far from the city.

LULA

Luís Inácio da Silva, better known as Lula or 'Squid' was born dirt poor in Brazil's northeast. As a boy, leaving his impoverished family and neighbours, he hitched a ride on a truck for the ten-day journey to São Paulo, Brazil's industrial giant, there to work firstly as a street child, shoeshine boy, then factory worker in the booming automobile business. He was regularly tear gassed for leading strikes but eventually his Worker Party propelled him to the presidency, his fourth attempt, in 2002, winning 60% of the vote and the hope of all Brazil.

Above: *Petrobrás' headquarters are located in downtown Rio.*

Tourism is important to Rio and great efforts have been made to protect it by, for example, deploying a special tourism police force and using English-language signs at popular tourist attractions.

Since 1997 Brazil's beef exports have jumped fivefold and President Lula has campaigned hard to force rich countries to reduce the trade barriers that are strangling all third-world agricultural exports. Trade with China has been rewarding, while production of automobiles and particularly bus bodies such as the Marco Polo variety that race along Rio's *avenidas*, plays a major role in the country's economy. Inflation was down to 9.3% in 2003 and the nation's trade surplus up to US$25 billion. The output of cereals and expansion of ranching, some of it on felled Amazon rainforest, has done much for exports although these are hampered by the roads: Brazil has 1,500,000km (937,500 miles) of roads of which only 11% are paved.

Lula's economic, fiscal and monetary plans to lower debt and inflation are not popular as they affect everyone's pocket. Even the 2004 increase in the minimum wage to R$285 (US$89) is not enough. Brazil, with China and India, is one of the three emerging world giants and is playing a larger role in world affairs. In 2004, 1200 Brazilian troops were in Haiti commanding a UN force, and Lula, wary of *Yanqui* imperialism, is often the spokesman for poor countries in the face of European and American hegemony. Brazil would like a seat on the UN Security Council and tends to play a mediating role in South American conflicts.

THE PEOPLE

A visitor to Rio was photographing a shoeshine boy humourously polishing the shoes of a bronze statue on Copacabana Promenade. The visitor rewarded the chirpy youngster with a few Reais. 'Is that all?' the shoeshine boy queried good-naturedly. The visitor showed his empty pockets. '*Tudo bem*,' (okay, fine) was the response and, grinning, he threw his arms around the visitor in a big hug. That is Rio de Janeiro and typical of the unaggressive and lighthearted approach of the Cariocas. They live to enjoy life, rain or shine, rich or poor. They wear slipslops to go shopping and love the feel of sand between their toes. They are never in a hurry (except when driving, whereupon a Formula-One gleam comes into their eyes) and will laughingly apologize for being two hours late for an appointment. They only get serious about football, samba and food. Strangely, they do not really think of themselves as South American or Latin American: merely, Brazilian.

They are extraordinarily kind to beggars, to children and always to gringos (foreigners), a word which is never meant derogatively. Perhaps it is the sunny climate or perhaps their history of slavery, poverty and isolation from the sterner Spanish countries around them. Or perhaps it is that they are a mix of so many colours and cultures. Nothing is ever a real problem, everything can be sorted out with a smile, a shrug and a little juggling of one's belt: *jogo de cintura*.

SOYA, RANCHING AND LOGGING

Brazil is hoping to pave the existing and economically vital 1765km (1097-mile) highway from **Cuiabá** in the Mato Grosso right through the Amazon Forest to **Santarém** in the north. BR-163, as the highway is known, could result in massive ecological damage, but not if Brazil's government can help it. They are intimately aware of the dangers and intend introducing strict ecological enforcement measures. With so much profit at stake, it will be a tough call.

Jogo de cintura

Unlike in the animal kingdom where each species lives in harmony with its neighbours, even if that is often eat and be eaten, we humans are often at odds with our fellow beings. Difference seems to divide us: wealth, accent, religion, gender, nationality, education and race. In spite of a history of slavery, Brazil has long considered itself a melting pot of races in which colour mattered not a jot. This is not entirely true. Racism was never institutionalized in Brazil but socially to be *preto* (black) or *pardo* (brown) was not always as comfortable as being

Below: *Young girls at Barra smile for the photographer.*

A WORD OR TWO

Indian words that have
migrated worldwide include:
jacaranda, piranha, tobacco,
potato, tapioca, maize and
toucan, the latter from the
cry the colourful bird makes.
Mango is a Malay and
Tamil word.

CITY SIGNS

• *Barco*:   Boat/ferry
• *Bairro*:   Neighbourhood
• *Bondinho*: Santa Teresa
                      train
• *Correio*:   Post office
• *Igreja*:   Church
• *Largo*:   A small square
• *Mirante*:   View point
• *Ônibus*:   Bus
• *Passagem*: Ticket
• *Praça*:   Square
• *Prefeitura*: Municipality
• *Rodoviária*: Bus station
NB Overhead street signs
show that block's numbers.

branco (white). Compared with many other countries, however, the mix has worked reasonably well for over a century. Some would like to see the country categorized into the above three divisions so that affirmative action, especially in deciding university places, can be implemented. Professor Peter Fry of Rio's Federal University sees this as a recipe for racial division and antagonism, especially in a country whose peoples have identified over 300 different categories for themselves.

Language

Brazilians speak **Portuguese**, but it is as different to the Portuguese of Continental Europe as Afrikaans is to Dutch. There are numerous accents and dialects, as one would expect in a country of 175 million people and a land that covers 8,500,000km² (3,281,850 square miles). Rio is over 5000km (3125 miles) from Manaus, the heart of the Amazon, further than London from Baghdad. Only Russia, Canada, China and the USA are larger than Brazil. There is not a great deal of **English** spoken in Rio (but probably more than in any other part of Brazil) and just a touch of other languages, especially **Spanish**. Everyone in Rio, with the exception of the pure indigenous Indian (and they live mainly in the Amazon), is a child of immigrants: Portuguese, Spanish, Swiss, African, Lebanese, German engineer, Italian factory worker, Japanese camera expert.

The Rio dialect is distinct even from São Paulo 430km (270 miles) away. 'Good day' is written *Bom dia*, but the 'd' becomes a 'g' in Rio. The words flow in liquid conjunction making it hard to understand as it is spoken so fast and with so many slang expressions. But open your phrase book and give it a go and you will rapidly win friends eager to try their English on you. Remember all 'r's are pronounced like an 'h' and 'o' is *ooh*. Portuguese is one of what is known as the Romance languages, derived from **Latin**, so if you speak a little Italian, Spanish, French or Romanian you'll get on. Only some 180 Indian languages still survive of the 700 thought to have been spoken when the Portuguese arrived. Nearly all of them are endangered.

Religion

In the folk memory of many black Brazilians, the world was born when everything was a wasteland of marsh and moving water, where only the lesser gods played on spider webs strung across the void. **Ol-orun**, the Most High, arranged for solid ground to be put in place, sent the chameleon with his big rolling eyes to observe it all and the world was created. Religion is important in Brazil. There are three main influences: Portuguese, Indian and African. The old time religion in Rio is **Roman Catholicism**. And it came with a sword in one hand and a cross in the other. Even the very first Indians who met Pedro Alvares Cabral near Porto Seguro on 22 April 1500 were encouraged to kneel before the *padrão* or stone cross of possession the Portuguese built.

Above: *Death, where is thy sting: dramatic art in Rio's cemetry.*
Opposite: *Sun, Samba and Africa blend in this beautiful girl's smile.*

About 1000 years ago Christendom split into two, Roman Catholicism and the Eastern Orthodox Church. Like all Christians, Catholics believe in Jesus Christ, the man-god who by his compassionate martyrdom redeemed humanity from what they believe is original sin. Over the millennia what was a simple community based religion developed into a powerful and wealthy worldwide institution led by a pope, cardinals and priests. **Catholicism** has produced some of the world's most beautiful music, sculpture and paintings, not least in many of Rio's churches. Cariocas are deeply immersed in Catholic culture (watch the footballers cross themselves as they run onto the pitch), but as with many city people it tends to be mothballed except for baptism, marriage and death. However, few Cariocas die atheist.

Evangelical and Pentecostal Christian churches in Rio have attracted many adherents, especially the young, with their music, intimacy and celebratory approach to worship. You will see their little churches in former shops along busy streets.

Islam and **Judaism**, the other two great Middle East religions, and partners with **Christianity** in 'the people of the book' are alive and well in Rio but their adherents are very much a minority.

THE SAINTS GO MARCHING IN

- **Yemanjá**: mother of the sea. She likes gifts of flowers.
- **Ogum**: the war *orixá*.
- **Oxúm**: *orixá* of families and love.
- **Exu** (Eshoo): looks like a black and red devil. Fond of rum.
- **Omolu**: the poor man's physician; has the power to cure.
- **Macumba**: a politically incorrect way of referring to Candomblé in Rio.
- **Oxumaré**: male god for six months of the year and female for the rest (one of two gods for homosexuals).
- **Quimbanda**: black magic. Taboo to even talk about it.

Above: *Spiritual guardian of the bay, Glória's 200-year-old royal chapel.*

Rio's 19th-century merchant princes fancied large *fazenda* estates, grand titles and even grander mansions. One such was **Francisco José da Rocha**, Baron of Itamaraty who made his fortune in coffee (black gold) and gemstones. He had a neoclassical palace built for him in 1859, but never lived in it. It was sold to the government in 1889 (the year the Republic was proclaimed), became the official presidential palace for a while, later the headquarters of the Ministry of Foreign Affairs and today is the **Historical and Diplomatic Museum** with one of the largest map collections in South America.

Indian religion is a religion of forest dwellers. Apart from Ol-orun it has many gods, among them **Tupan**, the fiery divinity of storms, lightning and thunder. Herbalists, psychotherapists and purveyors of spiritual gifts are known as *pagés*. The world around us and daily existence are the main influences of Indian religion, which down the centuries has all but disappeared under the onslaught of both Catholic and Protestant missionaries. Many of the great Christian orders came to Brazil to convert the native Indian, and the Jesuits in particular did much to protect them in their missions, from the depredations of slave raiders.

Afro-Brazilian religion as it is called has its origins in Nigeria, Ghana, and those other parts of Africa from where slaves were abducted. It is called **Candomblé** or **Umbanda**. Each person has an *orixá* (pronounced *orisha*) or two to guide and protect him, and this 'guardian angel' or god gives to the individual his or her personality. If you're not sure of your *orixá*, you need to visit (with suitable offerings and possibly animal sacrifice) a Candomblé priest (male or female) who will consult the cowrie shells and the ancestors. As in Africa the ceremonies are accompanied by dancing, singing and drumming and the *n'anga*, as they are called in Africa, will go into a trance. Advice, prediction and a general psychological cleansing result. Rio is particularly strong on Candomblé which for many years was banned, so the devotees gave their old gods the names of Christian saints to fool pious Catholics. As in everything else Cariocas are totally relaxed about religion.

Art, Sculpture and Architecture

Much of Rio's art is in its old colonial churches and monasteries such as **São Bento** or **Nossa Senhora da Gloria**. In the latter you will see superb examples of *azulejos* (white and blue Brazilian painted tiles), some based on Solomon's Song of Songs. The almost austere white and grey exteriors of Rio's colonial churches with their small village towers effectively disguise the incredible opulence of the gilded, minutely carved, painted and sculpted interiors. They say religion is what man has done to spirituality. Rio's old Baroque and Rococo churches are a phantasmagoria of gold, silver, wooden fretwork, patterns, statues, cherubs, angels, saints and sun-burst crosses. No inch is left uncovered by the piety of generations of artists and their wealthy patrons.

It was left to sculptor **Valentim de Fonseca e Silva** (1750–1813), affectionately known as Mestre Valentim, to add genius to the razzmatazz. His powerful works are in many churches and public areas in Rio. Try **São Francisco de Paula Church**. In 1816 a whole ship full of French craftsmen, artists, architects, sculptors and even musicians arrived in Rio and set up the **Imperial Academy**, influencing street design, churches, landscape and all the arts.

The **Museu do Indio** in Botafogo suburb shows the lifestyle and communal building techniques of the **Tupi-Guarani** who lived in temporary *ocas* made of branches in usually square *tabas*. The Portuguese navigators were taken aback. They had expected the vast edifices of the Aztecs and Incas.

Rio's colonial houses, white with brightly coloured windows and shutters and red roof tiles, were built with thick walls supported by a wooden frame in which a mix of dung, clay, and vegetable fibre was poured, each layer being allowed to dry. A *sobrado* house had more than one storey (then everyone knew you had money), and courtyards were private interior squares similar to monastic cloisters. This style of construction hardly changed in 300 years. Neoclassical buildings after the French style, including the **Museu Nacional** and **Institute Benjamín Constant**, were constructed when the Portuguese royal family fled to Rio. In 1906 Rio tried hard to become the Paris of the tropics with

Below: *The daunting solidity of the Museu Nacional in the gardens of Quinta da Boa Vista.*

the construction of a Renoir Boulevard in the form of **Avenida Rio Branco**, destroying many old houses in the process, then, using what is called the Eclectic style, constructing such impressive edifices as the **Opera House** and the **National Library**.

Most of Rio's modern architecture, of which there is not a great deal other than the beachfront condominiums and frenetic California shopping malls in Barra, was put in place by such visionary Brasilian architects as **Oscar Niemeyer** and landscape designer, **Roberto Burle Marx**.

Film and TV

Juliana Paes is one of the top stars of *telenovelas* (soaps), many of which are made in Rio at **Rede Globo Studios** and are watched avidly each evening throughout Brazil. Many have been exported. They are often semi-historical, dramatic if somewhat predictable, of a high quality, and everyone is beautiful. Rio has always been the home of Brazilian movies. Bossa nova and Carnaval swept the world when Marcel Camus' *Black Orpheus* was released in 1958. Hector Babenco's 1981 film *Pixote* about a street child from the *favelas* in Rio won the Cannes Palme d'Or, while Bruno Barreto's *Four Days in September* based on the kidnapping of the US ambassador to Brazil was nominated for an Oscar in 1998. The recent and poignant Rio Central Station story of a poor peoples' street letter writer and her search for a little boy's father in *Me, You, Them* popularized the northeast accordion dance music *forró*.

The Magic of Music

Rio is not all samba. There is plenty of **classical orchestral music** at, in particular, the Municipal Theatre, the Salo Maestro Armando Prazeres-Bennett, the Sala Cecília Meireles, and at such venues as Candelária Church and the Teatro do Centro Cultural Banco do Brasil (CCBB). Local and world-famous artists are featured, the *Viva Musica!* organizers issue a monthly diary and Rio has its own Philharmonic Orchestra.

Big popular musical events are of course **Carnaval** in February, the **Winter Festival** in Petrópolis and the **Rio in Concert Festival** in the nearby mountain town of Teresópolis in September, a fabulous costume party.

On **New Year's Eve** up to two million people wassail on Copacabana Beach and watch the fireworks. You will often see impromptu singalongs at Rio's bars. In Centro, street musicians include the excellent blind pianist **Glaucia Leite**.

Above: *Playboy cover girl and soap star Juliana Paes.*
Opposite : *Chilean street band in downtown Rio.*

Literature: The Noble Art

José de Alencar's (1829–77) novel reflects an idealistic Indian way of life not unlike Gauguins' South Pacific paintings or Rousseau's altruistic writings. **Joaquim Maria Machado de Assis** (1839–1908), a mulatto, as the term used to be, wrote hundreds of short stories and nine novels, several of which were covert attacks on slavery and nearly all of which were set in Rio. Founder of the Brazilian Academy of Letters, he is probably Brazil's greatest writer. **Carlos Drummond de Andrade** (1902–87) is Brazil's best-loved poet. His *Travelling in the Family* is available in English. Ukrainian-born **Clarice Lispector**'s (1920–77) moving novels were often set in middle-class Rio and nearly always featured women as the central characters. Her *Family Ties* is published by the University of Texas Press. **Paulo Coelho**, who wrote *The Alchemist*, is known worldwide, while **Jorge Amado**'s (1912–2001) romances are hugely popular.

There are well-stocked bookshops in every *bairro* of Rio, usually with a small English section. A particularly good one is **Copa Books**, Rua Francisco Sá, 26. Lj.A. Copacabana. Corner kiosks sell newspapers and a variety of magazines.

QUEENS OF SOAP

Telenovelas or soaps are the opiate of Rio. Every night everybody everywhere watches them. A recent star is the black and beautiful 26-year-old Tais Araujo, while even more famous is the Carnaval favourite Juliana Paes, 25-year-old actress from Niterói across Guanabara Bay. Juliana achieved fame in the soap *Celebrity* and, uncovered, on the cover of *Playboy*.

A THOUSAND CHOICES

SAARA is the Portuguese acronym for the Society of Friends of Rua da Alfadega neighbourhood, a crowded almost Persian market in Centro where vendors shout for your custom, prices are low, you have a choice of 1250 stores, and the Arab, Israeli and Korean food is exotic.

Tastes of the Tropics

You should not leave Rio without sampling the traditional *feijoada completa,* originally the basic dish that slaves ate because they had nothing else. It is a spiced-up black-bean stew cooked with smoked sausages, salt pork, sun-dried beef and other meats. *Farofa* (manioc flour) is shaken on top and the whole delicious monster is eaten with kale cabbage leaves, rice and orange slices. Family Saturday lunch is *feijoada* day. It goes on for most of the afternoon especially if a good *cachaça* rum is served. Then it's time for a nap.

Light meals at corner bars can be enormously rewarding and cheap in Rio. Try *galetto* (game hen) or the Argentinian origin *churrascaria* (mixed-grill barbecue). Eat as much as you like of such delicacies as *cavaquinha* (a lobster dish), paper-thin pizzas, spicy Bahian dishes or *comida mineiro* specialities from neighbouring Minas Gerais province.

Everybody drinks **Pilsener** in Rio. It is called **chopp**. Countless pavement bars or *chopperia* serve it ice cold in small glass after glass.

Where to Eat

The best atmosphere, the best beer and often the best food in Rio are usually found in what are called **botequins** (taverns). There are at least 60 of these venerable and popular places in Rio, usually in older buildings. They are family run and have been for decades. They serve house specialities (often to live music) that are incomparable. Try **Jobi** in Leblon (Av Ataulfo de Paiva) or **Na Pressão** in Barra da Tijuca (Av Mal Henrique Lott). For the best and coldest *chopp* draft try **Bar Luiz** (Rua da Carioca) in Centro or **Bar Brasil** in Lapa (Av Mem de Sá).

There are Lebanese, Portuguese, Italian, French, Chinese, Sushi, Indian and vegetarian **restaurants**. A

HOPPING FOR FOOD

- Coconut milk: *leite de coco*
- Black beans: *feijão preto*
- Tea: *chá*
- Butter: *manteiga*
- Cheese: *queijo*
- Bread: *pão*
- Sugar: *açúcar*
- Rice: *arroz*

GREAT LOOS

Any restaurant will let you use their loo. The word is *banheiro,* pronounced banyehro. There are good facilities at airports, Rio's central bus station, Sugar Loaf and Corcovado but nothing at metro stops. The best loos and showers in town are at the big numbered lifeguard towers along Ipanema and Copacabana promenades. You pay R$1 and are given packeted tissue and soap. The English notice at the entrance includes the thoughtful admonition: 'Do pee in the toilet'.

favourite and inexpensive way of eating is at a **por-kilo** or **a-quilo** restaurant. You take what you like of salads and meats, have it all weighed and pay accordingly. You'll see them in every street. **Lanchonetes** are inexpensive snack bars where you can get such tasties as *empada* (pie). Many restaurants serve a table-d'hôte meal called *prato feito* or *sortido*. You can even get Bob's Burgers, but they're not all that cheap. If you can afford it, breakfast at the elegant **Copacabana Palace Hotel** is an experience.

The main meal in Rio is taken in the middle of the day. If you like **fruit**, go for *guaraná* which all will assure you is an aphrodisiac. Then there is the star-shaped carambola, cajú, mango, custard apple, acerola and the ubiquitous guava, from which incidentally a tasty ketchup is made.

Rum, Lime and Sugar

Bohemia is an adjective often used in Rio to describe older, arty and interesting neighbourhoods. It is also the name of the best bottled **Pilsener**. Bohemia started making its delicious brew in 1853. But there are plenty of others: Atlantica, Skol, Brahma and Itaipara. **Lager** is rare; there is a guiness – like black Xingu beer – but no English ales. Draft, chilled Pilsener or *chopp* is by far the favourite drink in hot Rio. *Guaraná* is a popular fizzy drink as are non-alcoholic *sucos* fruit drinks at street corners. Iced coconut water sipped from the nut is the beach-promenade tipple. You can try the strong *maté* tea of the cowboys, but if you want English tea ask for cold milk, *leite frio*. *Cachaça* or *batida* is Brazil's staple white sugar-cane rum. It is the same word in Portuguese-influenced Africa where it is much rougher. The best way to drink it is shaken with limes, crushed ice and castor sugar. The result is called *caipirinha*. Beware, gringo!

Haute Foods

One-hundred-year-old *belle-époque* elegance still blooms at Confeitaria Colombo Restaurant in the heart of Old Rio, a favourite downtown attraction for connoisseurs of *art nouveau* and *haute cuisine*. Opened in 1894 when French impressionist Renoir was at the peak of his genius, the open double-storey salons of the restaurant are lined with ornate jacaranda-framed mirrors imported from Belgium at the turn of the century, while the showcases, furniture, fittings, ceiling lights and floor all date back to an era when ladies took afternoon tea and gentlemen carried ivory-handled canes.

Opposite: *Freshly squeezed* sucos *fruit juice for every taste.*
Below: *Superb beer, service, food and TV football at pavement corner cafés.*

2
Rio Centro

Rio de Janeiro's downtown area is not a Sunday shopping city. It is practically deserted, but if you go in a group with a good guide you'll be able to have a traffic-free walkabout through 500 years of historical hideaways, colonial churches, monuments and lovely tree-filled squares.

You can visualize yourself coming in from the sea with **Sugar Loaf** on your left, **Santos Dumont Airport** ahead and Niterói's 14km (9-mile) bridge on your right. You 'land' at **Praça Quinze** which used to be the sailing ship mud flats port when the original Rio settlement on Urca was transferred in 1567 to **Morro do Castelo**, a hill that was shovelled away in the 1920s. Today, Praça Quinze features all-day folk-art markets on Thursdays and Fridays.

PRAÇA 15 DE NOVEMBRO

There are probably more historic buildings in and around Praça 15 de Novembro than anywhere else in Rio de Janeiro. Start at the ancient pyramid-shaped *Chafariz* (water fountain) designed in 1789, the year of the French Revolution, by creative genius **Mestre Valentim**, whose mother was a slave and whose father was apparently a Portuguese nobleman. This water fountain, one of several, was a natural meeting point for 'tiger slaves' (so called because of the urine and night soil they carried in buckets on their heads), a place where servant girls chatted and ships renewed their supplies.

Opposite: *Arcos da Lapa. Go by train over this 250-year-old aqueduct.*

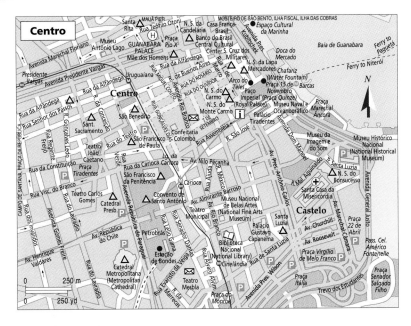

Paço Imperial **

In a corner of the square is the **Paço Imperial** (Royal Palace), a vast 1743 three-storey tiled complex with art exhibits, bookstore, theatre, cinema and restaurants. Originally the governor's residence, then the armoury, it was a palace from 1808 when the Portuguese court re-sited itself in Brazil, until the Republic was proclaimed in 1889. A model of the city and an exhibit demonstrating the original construction of Paço Imperial are worth seeing.

BEYOND PRAÇA 15 DE NOVEMBRO
Ilha Fiscal and Ilha das Cobras *

From Praça 15 de Novembro you'll see the **Beau Geste Castle** on **Ilha Fiscal** just off shore, palms fluttering in the breeze. Supposedly built as a customs house, its fairytale cuteness so charmed the emperor he decided it should only be opened for parties. The much larger island, **Ilha das Cobras**, with its three old forts flanks Fiscal Island. Cobra is an original Portuguese word meaning snake.

BOMBEIROS

The general headquarters of Rio's fire department or Corpo de Bombeiros in the Praça da República is pure Disneyland: smiling porthole turrets, white column upon column, dozens of high windows, coats of arms, and a central ice-cream square tower. All in pink adobe. It is, of course, in the eclectic style and was built in 1905 to house Brazil's first military conscription office.

Mosteiro de São Bento **

The hilltop **Mosteiro de São Bento** (Monastery of St Benedict) is not far from Praça 15. **St Benedict**, a monk who lived 1500 years ago, founded the rule upon which Christian monasticism is based (community work, meditation, plain chant). Outside in front of the modest twin bell towers is a small quiet square of trees; inside, the small church justifies its status as a Unesco World Heritage Site. Exquisite marble and marquetry dating back 400 years cover the roof and sides with gold leaf and red paint on wood, in an exotic Baroque praise to God. With the chandeliers lit, it is dazzling to the point where one is distracted from the haunting Latin of the black-hooded monks as they process in to choir and begin that Gregorian plainchant that has so caught the imagination of our modern era. **Frei Ricardo do Pilar**'s masterpiece *O Salvador* hangs in the sacristy.

Espaço Cultural da Marinha *

The narrow, cobbled streets of **Travessa do Comércio** and **Arco do Teles** just off Praça 15 are an area of period pastel-coloured façades, filigree street lamps and jam-packed happy-hour bars and restaurants. **Rua do Ouvídor** (Justices of the Peace) was originally a 16th-century pathway. If you like ships, visit the **Espaço Cultural da Marinha**. Specialities include the World War II torpedo boat *Bauru*, the modern submarine *Riachuelo* and the *Galeota*, the royal family's sailboat 180 years ago.

STREET NIBBLES

Apart from the traffic bustle, Centro is full of colourful street markets and characters. Peddlers selling fast food, *pacoquinha* (pressed peanut powder chunks), *cicadas* (sweet coconut cookies), *danoninho* (tiny jars of yoghurt), *pão de queijo* (cheese puffs), *churros* (caramel in deep-fried dough sprinkled with cinnamon sugar), *bolinho de Aipim* (mincemeat in fried cassava dough) and everywhere corn-on-the-cob.

CHURCHES OF CENTRO

There are at least 15 historic churches packed into Centro. They include **Santa Cruz dos Militares** dating back to 1628 with its interior decorated by Mestre Valentim, the 1611 **Carmo Convent**, and the **Church of Our Lady of the Third Order of Carmelites** again featuring Valentim, possibly as something of a snub to the other Carmelite convent. In the Rua do Ouvídor is the small 18th-century Baroque masterpiece, **Igreja de Nossa Senhora da Lapa dos Mercadores** (Church of Our Lady of Lapa, patron of Peddlers). The tower bells of São José ring pleasantly over the city as you church hunt.

Left: *Arco do Teles. Restored and preserved 250-year-old Colonial Rio.*

Os Lusiades

Luis Vaz de Camões (1524–80) is Portugal's great epic poet. He lived at the time of Portugal's incredible maritime journeys and experienced at least one himself by rounding Africa's Cape of Good Hope. Some would say his *Os Lusíades* poem is comparable with Milton's *Paradise Lost*, Danté's *Inferno* and even Homer's *Odyssey*. There is an original first edition of Camões' poem in Centro's **Real Gabinete Português de Leitura**, the second largest library in Rio.

Below: *Rio's Opera House, Teatro Municipal.*

Banco do Brasil Central Cultural Center **

The six-storey **Banco do Brasil Central Cultural Center** has eight well-appointed exhibition rooms, two theatres, a cinema, bookshop, library, lunch-time concerts, video cabins, restaurant and teashop. A recent exhibition was *Yanomami. Soul of the Amazon*, a haunting portrayal in black and white pictures by 11 photographers with sound, light, commentary and music about the few surviving Yanomami Indians. At the centre you will nearly always find theatre reflecting some aspect of Brazilian dance, as well as Shakespeare.

Adjacent to the entrance to the cultural centre, still in Presidente Vargas Street, is the 1920 **Casa França-Brasil**, the first neoclassical building to be constructed in Rio.

AVENIDA RIO BRANCO AND SURROUNDS

Along Avenida Rio Branco, which was built in 1906 in a fit of Parisian boulevard enthusiasm and which cuts right through downtown Rio from Mauá Pier to Gloria suburb, is a cluster of grand edifices.

Teatro Municipal *

The Teatro Municipal is not unlike the famous Opéra in Paris: cupolas, Grecian columns, iron grillwork arches, high windows, sloping slate roofs, statues and soaring eagles. It was constructed in the weird and wonderful style known as eclectic, combining neoclassic forms and lavish *belle-époque* decoration. The interior is even more glitzy with Carrara marble staircases, gold leaf and sparkling chandeliers. It seats precisely 2357 opera lovers. You can book for a tour of the theatre.

Museu Nacional de Belas Artes *

Opposite the theatre is the equally eclectic 1906–08 **Museu Nacional de Belas Artes** (National Fine Arts Museum). One gallery is devoted to Brazilian artists over

Left: *Largo da Carioca seen from Santo Antonio Church – flowering trees, street nibbles and lots of people action.*

the past 400 years. The interior corridor, inspired by the Louvre in Paris, is flanked by a gauntlet of Grecian statues. There are 20,000 exhibits in the museum.

Biblioteca Nacional ★

Rare manuscripts and some 10 million volumes are housed in the great Corinthian-columned 100-year-old **Biblioteca Nacional** (National Library) which started with the collection King John VI brought with him from Portugal in 1808. French stained-glass windows and skylights give it an airy, almost ethereal feel.

Largo da Carioca ★★

Largo da Carioca, which many will say is the communal heart of Rio, is surrounded by a little park, stalls, street vendors and the Petrobrás skyscraper. It is overlooked by the hilltop **Igreja e Convento de Santo Antônio** (Church and Monastery of Saint Anthony), which came into existence in 1592 as a tiny meditation hermitage for the Franciscans. **Saint Anthony** was an Egyptian hermit-mystic or desert father who lived 1700 years ago. The Baroque interior featuring the life of the saint in oils and blue Brazilian tiles is sumptuous. It is, in fact, two churches. **Friar Vincente do Salvador**, author in 1627 of the first history of Brazil was a monk here. It's a good place to picnic beneath the flamboyant trees and you can get snacks in the church forecourt sold by the good ladies of the parish. A lift takes you up to the church and there's a small museum of sacred Christian art.

Above: *Rio's huge Metro-politan Cathedral can accommodate a congregation of 20,000 people.*
Opposite: *Downtown Rio. Busy, bustling, booming.*

Nossa Senhora da Candelária **

Greco-Roman architecture is known in the West as neo-classical. It involves many grand columns. On the Praça Pio X is the neoclassical 1775–1810 church **Nossa Senhora da Candelária** (Our Lady of Candelária). It was built on the site of a 1610 chapel by Leonor and Antônio Marins de Gonçalves Palma, who promised God that they would build such a chapel if they survived the storm that was threatening to capsize them in Guanabara Bay. They survived and they did. Their story is narrated in paintings inside the dome of this exquisite church. Surrounded by modern city blocks it sits astride Av Presidente Vargas, its dome and twin flanking towers easily seen from a distance.

Metropolitan Cathedral **

Sebastian, or rather Sebastião, is the patron saint of Rio and a favourite name for boys. Sebastian was a 3rd-century Christian saint martyred by being shot with arrows and then beaten to death in gory Roman style. The largest church in Rio is named after him.

Rio's ultra-modern **Metropolitan Cathedral** is truly awesome. It resembles an Aztec temple – a round pyramid tapering up and then leveled at 83m (270ft). It can easily accommodate a congregation of 5000 seated or 20,000 standing, and the elevated altar is large enough to seat an entire orchestra.

Its concrete panelled exterior is divided by four stained-glass panels, each 60m (200ft) high and as wide as two buses. You can stroll round the hushed interior and listen to the gentle lament of Gregorian chant coming from the slim loudspeakers. The cathedral was built 30 years ago but after all this time the stained-glass panels are still giving problems.

REBEL TOOTH-PULLER

Tiradentes, the tooth-puller, would today be called a freedom fighter. He was gruesomely executed for leading a revolt against the government. The **Palácio Tiradentes**, the Legislative Assembly of Rio State, is named after him. Fluted Grecian columns topped with Homeric statues mark the entrance to this huge building in Rua Prímeiro de Março. A national hero, Tiradentes was incarcerated in the prison that used to occupy this precise spot. There is also the **Praça Tiradentes** in Rio Centro, not far from the cathedral.

THE HISTORICAL AREA

At Praça Marechal Âncora are the last remnants of Rio's original 16th-century settlement on Morro do Castelo. The ancient church of **Nossa Senhora do Bonsucesso** (Our Lady of Good Luck) marks the spot where a rather forlorn cobbled path, called appropriately Ladeira da Misericórdia (Slope of Mercy), creeps upwards past shuttered buildings. It is Rio's oldest street.

Museu Histórico Nacional ★★

In contrast to the poverty of the *ladeira* is the **Museu Histórico Nacional** (National Historical Museum),in the Praça Marechal Âncora. This red-tiled colonial building contains 250,000 exhibit items depicting the history of the royal family, slavery, horse-drawn coaches, the largest coin collection in South America, maps, armour, colonial furniture, works of art and porcelain. It was here that prisoners and runaway slaves were incarcerated and probably tortured in the old *Calabouço* (calaboose) of 1693. In 1762, the armoury, Casa do Trem, was added. The quartered remains of the rebel and martyr **Tiradentes** were initially kept here. Rio's Legislative Assembly building in Centro is also named after this charismatic but doomed revolutionary.

CAMPO DE SANTANA ★

Campo de Santana in the Praça da República is the largest public garden and green lung in downtown Rio. It is off the Avenida Presidente Vargas, the carriageway that bisects Centro from west to east, and you can get to it by taking the metro to Central Railway Station. The gardens with their lakes and swans are surrounded by a host of historical buildings reflecting the rise and fall of the Brazilian Empire. They include the **Casa de Deodoro**, former residence of **Marechal Deodoro da Fonseca**, who became the first president of Brazil in 1889.

NOSSA SENHORA CHURCHES

- Nossa Senhora da Lapa dos Mercadores (1747).
- Nossa Senhora do Ordem Tercera do Carmo (1755).
- Nossa Senhora do Carmo, antiga Sé (1761).
- Nossa Senhora do Bonsucesso (began as a 16th-century chapel).
- Nossa Senhora da Candelária (1775).

WAR WITH PARAGUAY

No one can quite remember why Brazil spent five years (1865–70) fighting her neighbour Paraguay other than the provocative machinations of Paraguayan President Francisco Solana López. It was to prove costly for him: Paraguay was virtually annihilated by the combined armies of Brazil, Argentina and Uruguay leaving only 28,000 men and 200,000 women alive. General Manuel Luiz Osório led the Brazilian forces and it is his equestrian statue we see today in Praça Quinze.

3
Sugar Loaf Mountain, Urca and Botafogo

Sugar Loaf Mountain or **Pão de Açúcar** rears like a giant artillery shell out of the Atlantic mist guarding Rio's Guanabara Bay. Named after the almond-shaped mould used to refine cane sugar, alternately the Indian word for hill, the mountain sits in the middle of **Urca** suburb. Like the *Cristo Redentor* facing it 8km (5 miles) away across **Botafogo**, it is visible from nearly everywhere in Rio.

SUGAR LOAF MOUNTAIN ★★★

Sugar Loaf's granite peak is 394m (1293ft) high. The luxurious full-visibility cable car reaches it in twin-peak stages and has been doing so since 1912. Operating every 30 minutes, the first *caminho aéreo* leaves at 08:15 and the last down descends at 22:00. The new Italian-built cable cars, carrying up to 75 passengers, are amazingly stable and quick. You can't miss the terminus at **Praia Vermelha** in Urca and there is very little queuing. You will want to use your camera on the 1325m (1450yd) ascent.

The first stage takes you to **Morro da Urca** (Urca Peak) at 218m (715ft), which surprisingly has been converted into a huge multifaceted visitor platform, complete with helicopter pad for sightseeing trips, café, restaurant, nightclub, outdoor amphitheatre, children's playground and curio shops. Towards evening, parts of the platform are cordoned off to provide for small cocktail parties. The views of course are stunning, as the lush jungle and granite mountainside falls sheer to **Botafogo Bay** with its flotillas of yachts, and across to lovely **Flamengo** bayside park further north.

DON'T MISS

★★★ **Sugar Loaf :** an icon of Rio de Janeiro.
★★ **Vermelha Beach:** shady trees and promenade.
★★ **Urca Walkabout:** Rio's original 1565 settlement.
★ **General Tibúrcio Square:** monumental statuary to long-gone wars.
★ **Museu do Índio:** one of Botafogo's museums.
★ **São João Batista Cemetery:** tearful tomb art.

Opposite: *Beach, bay and towering Sugar Loaf Mountain.*

Above: *Take a ride in the sky up to Sugar Loaf with Copa beach below.*

FLYCATCHER PATH

Tucked into the one corner of **Vermelha Beach** is a kindergarten school. Alongside it is the sea-flanking Cláudio Coutinho or more colloquially Flycatcher Path (Caminho do Bem-te-vi), leading up to the foot of Sugar Loaf. You can easily reach the cable car's first stage on Urca Rock from this path by turning left some 350m (382 yards) from the school then through the forest. The experts will inform you that there are 35 rock-climb routes to Sugar Loaf summit itself.

Signs admonish you not to feed the animals but don't expect to come across jaguars or boa constrictors.

The next stage (each takes about 10 minutes) glides up to Sugar Loaf itself. The circular balustrade here is smaller than the one at Urca Peak but the panoramic views are even more stupendous. You can see practically the whole of Rio as it meanders along the blue shores far below. You might have to jostle a little for photo opportunities as this is one of the world's great sights and there are always plenty of visitors, particularly during Carnaval. If you want to get away from all the tourists take the steps down to the path that winds through the bamboo jungle. There are seats at each good view and you're quite likely to be on your own, gazing out over Guanabara Bay and Niterói. In the distant haze, 50km (31 miles) away, is the **Serra do Mar** – a long line of blue mountains embracing and framing Rio. You will be amazed to recognize flowers and trees now common in many other parts of the tropical and semitropical world. To the right of the cable car, the *Redentor* is easily visible as it is nearly twice as high as Sugar Loaf. Evening, as the lights of Rio begin to twinkle, is magical. Position one of the chairs to the left or right of the cable-car platform and indulge. You might have to compete with a TV crew because wherever you go in Rio, someone always seems to be shooting a commercial. The sun sets behind the far mountains and as if on cue the city centre, Glória, Botafogo and along the coasts, Copacabana and Ipanema light up beneath the seaside granite domes. At the top you can buy a snack, a T-shirt or even an emerald pendant.

Sugar Loaf should be your first place to visit in Rio, not because it is necessarily the most attractive, but because with a map to hand, you can quickly familiarize yourself with the geography of the city. Standing with the Atlantic at your back **Copa** is on your left, and 50km (31 miles) further is the coastal road to **São Paulo**, **Iguaçu Falls** and **Argentina**. In front of you is downtown Rio and to your far right the twin, but much smaller city of Niterói which leads onto **Bahia** and **Salvador** and north 3500km (2100 miles) to the mouth of the **Amazon** and the **West Indies**.

URCA **
Red Sand and Chopin

Urca lies at the base of Mount Urca. The residential suburb was built around a series of improvised buildings occupied by the military. You may be fortunate enough to see the changing of the guard on **General Tibúrcio Square** with its fountains, colourful gardens and multifaceted memorial to heroes killed in the 19th-century war with Brazil's neighbour Paraguay (*see* panel, page 37). The monument is nearly 70 years old.

Bordering the monument and shaded by coconut palms and the ubiquitous *badam* trees, **Vermelha Promenade** faces a small beach of unusually claret-tinged sand, hence Vermelha. Here you can sip an iced coconut, have a snack at the cannon-flanked **Círculo Militar da Praia Vermelha** restaurant and admire the pensive statue of **Chopin** given to the city by Rio's Polish immigrants. It was moved downtown to Cinelândia and the Municipal Theatre at one stage. All Urca protested and it was hurriedly reinstated.

Day and night, fishermen perch on the great slide of Carioca granite known as *pedra de galho* that stretches down to the beach. Glance over your shoulder and you'll see professional climbers roped to the vertical rock face of **Babylon Hill** above the cable car station.

Pastiche of Pastel Houses *

Urca dates back to 1565. A small settlement at the entrance to **Guanabara Bay**, which in the next century was to become **Fortaleza São João**. Urca has been a major military area ever since and is still in some ways cut off from mainstream Rio.

An ideal walk is to go from **Praia Vermelha Promenade** back along **Avenida Pasteur** and then swing north past the rows of pretty houses snuggling up to the granite heights. The houses are built in every possible pastel colour and style. The

---

PÃO DE AÇÚCAR

The word sugar comes from the ancient Indian Sanskrit word sárkarã or çucre in old French. Sugar cane, the 2m (6ft) tall pipes which when crushed and the juice refined, yields the sweet-tooth crystals Western Europe has always craved. It was the first commercial crop in Rio as the lush, wet coastal soil was ideal for water-hungry cane, especially around the river mouths, and there was easy sea access to European ports. It was grown initially with Indian slave labour but when they resisted, African slaves were imported. Brazil is the world's largest exporter of sugar and this is reflected in their national drink, **caipirinha**, a white rum-based firewater made with sliced limes, crushed ice and castor sugar. Divine.

Below: *Praia Vermelha. Claret sands and Indian almond trees near Sugar Loaf cable car terminal.*

SAINTS ALIVE

There are few signs of Islam, Judaism, Buddhism and Hinduism in Rio. Naturally enough, as the city's main religious antecedents are Southern European Christianity and African mysticism both of which have been finely syncretized into a local religion known as **Candomblé** which the slaves developed, adapting Roman Catholic saints to disguise their old African gods.

GENTLE ANCHORAGE

A lovely bridge marks the corner of **Quadrado da Urca**, the tranquil harbour where hand-line fishermen anchor their small colourful boats in Urca. Seabirds dive looking for fish scraps, the air is fresh and Corcovada can be clearly seen across the city.

Below: *Man-made Urca beach is a good place to go for a swim.*

neighbourhood grew on top of landfill and its well-heeled plastic surgeons, senior military officers and decorous security make it the one suburb Cariocas would love to live in. Architectural styles vary from Elizabethan beams, Normandy castles, Greek columns, Mexican haciendas and even a Chinese pagoda.

You can swim at the man-made **Praia da Urca** in front of the old and now derelict 1930s **Casino Hotel** where **Carmen Miranda**, the exotic singer and Hollywood star performed (*see* panel, page 43).

Along Avenida Pasteur, the only access road to Urca, are several handsome 19th-century buildings including the Economics and Journalism Campus of the **Federal University of Rio** (once a mental asylum), the **Institute Benjamin Constant** for blind children and the **Earth Science Museum** fronted by a great white lion and eagle.

BOTAFOGO *

The *bairro* (suburb or neighbourhood) of Botafogo lies behind Copacabana halfway between Sugar Loaf and the *Redentor*. It was developed when the tramway was built to link Botafogo Bay with Lake Rodrigo de Freitas and the nearby Botanical Gardens.

One of the most interesting spots in Botafogo, believe it or not, is the large cemetery of **São João Batista** off the crowded and motor-spares street of Rua General Polidoro. A lofty entrance arch leads left, right and centre along sun-dappled leafy pathways flanked by the beautiful, pious, sentimental and occasionally grotesque

mausoleums and statues of Rio's wealthy departed. Along smaller paths behind them are more modest mementos featuring signed tombs, sepia pictures of lost ones and Roman Catholic influenced sculpture. Saint John and Mary at the foot of Christ's Calvary cross is a favourite. Yellow-flowered trees and creeper abound. Above you on the hill are the small white cabinets of the poor while

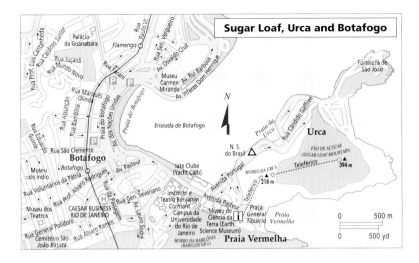

Sugar Loaf, Urca and Botafogo

on the opposite hill is a small *favela*. Appropriately, the *Redentor* is clearly visible on Corcovado Mount.

Yacht Clubs *

Rio Yacht Club, founded ninety years ago, lies tucked into the lea of Av Portugal off Av Pasteur. Listen carefully and you will hear the lanyards of moored yachts tinkling in the breeze, and when the wind freshens, yachts tack and go about in sparkling display. Further along is the **Guanabara Regatta Club**. Right on the seafront with a clear view of the yachting action and Sugar Loaf, is the 'noble' **Rio Sole Mar** (Sea and Sun) restaurant with prawns, dozens of tables, dancing and a violin orchestra.

Museu do Índio *

There are some 60 museums in Rio. In Botafogo, one of the most interesting is the **Museu do Índio**, a typical Botafogo townhouse with true-to-life garden displays of Indian dwellings, musical instruments, costumes, baskets, weapons, masks and a vast reservoir of documents, pictures, sound recordings and works on indigenous Indian ethnology. The **Museu dos Teatros**, tracing the history of theatre in Rio, is also worth a visit.

CARMEN MIRANDA

Ronald Reagan would have known the scintillating **Carmen Miranda**. The whole world did. Samba dancer, singer and Cleopatra of camp, she stormed onto Broadway (with comedy pair **Abbot** and **Costello**), then Hollywood in the 1940s. Born in Portugal in 1909, she lived at 131 Av São Sebastião on the Guanabara-facing side of Urca with its squares and yellow-flowering Mimosa trees. She died of a heart attack at 46, some say of sadness after the way Rio society treated her when she returned home from the USA. Her full name was **Maria do Carmo Miranda da Cunha**.

4
Santa Teresa

It is probably true to say that when a Carioca is young, passionate and artistic, he or she yearns to live in Santa Teresa. The cool little olde-worlde hilltop village of Santa Teresa sits right in the middle of Rio, overlooking *favelas* and the bustling city below, and is named after the 16th-century Spanish Carmelite mystic and writer, Teresa of Ávila, possibly the greatest female intellectual in the Christian Church. Mount Carmel itself is in biblical Palestine.

Santa Teresa's colonial 19th-century buildings twist up along higgledy-piggledy cobbled, tree-lined streets inhabited mainly by artists, craft-makers and Bohemians. The hill was first called **Desterro** (exile) after a hermitage built there in 1624 by reclusive **Antônio Gomes do Desterro**.

The Santa Teresa Convent *
The convent was built in 1750. There is limited access to the huge white and grey Rococo (the elaborate and graceful 18th-century architecture that originated in France) convent up the *ladeira* (pathway) of mossy stones flanked by little colonial houses. The Carmelite Sisters are a contemplative 'enclosed' order. But individual sisters counsel visitors (Carmelites are famed worldwide for their spiritual guidance) while 08:00 Sunday mass with the cloistered sisters singing unseen is balm to the soul. Rarely open to the public is the convent's fabulous collection of paintings, statuary and manuscripts, preserved by the National Historical and Artistic Institute.

Don't Miss

*** **The Little Train:** take a ride to Santa Teresa on the *bondinho* tram.
** **Escadaria Selarón:** patterns made with thousands of colourful ceramic tiles cover this impressive staircase.
* **Santa Teresa Convent:** a lovely 18th-century Rococo building.
* **La Vereda Shop:** crafts made from old wood.
** **Santa Teresa Walks:** ideal way to explore the Bohemian streets.

Opposite: *Fairytale castle in the sky residence in Santa Teresa built in 1879.*

Right: *Cadging a ride on the* bondinho *up Santa Teresa.*

The Little Train ***

The most exciting way to reach Santa Teresa is in one of the old open-sided yellow ***bondinhos*** (trams) which grind and rattle their way up the circuitous tracks every 30 minutes, young locals clinging on to the sides and

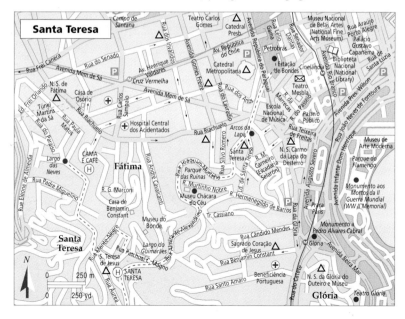

travelling free. The original streetcars were pulled by donkeys 150 years ago. The word *bondinho* comes from the bonds or securities used to float the first electric tram companies in Rio.

Your journey starts at Lélio Gama Street off Senador Dantas Street, not far from Cinelândia Metro Station, behind the Petrobrás building. There are two train routes. Take the Paula Matos line. The first thrill is going high above the city on the Roman-like aqueduct, the 250-year-old **Arcos da Lapa** on which the railway track was laid on 1 September 1896. The train slows, jerks and screeches to a halt after crossing the Arcos.

Escadaria Selarón **

Santa Teresa is postcard perfect. Take a walk around to the **Ladeira Santa Teresa** and further up to the convent. Keep going and you'll come to the spectacular and hugely colourful steps of **Escadaria Selarón** (Selarón's Staircase) made with thousands of chipped ceramic tiles in all designs and colours and from all over the world, that adorn the 215 steps.

Selarón – the artist whose idea it was – still sits here changing the odd tile when someone sends him one. The *escadaria* is also known as **Escada da Rua Manuel Carneiro** after the street from which it ascends. It's quite a guitar and folksy spot, not unlike the Spanish Steps in Rome.

Castles in the Sky **

Yellow fever, the mosquito-born tropical disease, was the curse of Rio in centuries past. Many came to live in breeze-refreshed Santa Teresa to escape the clutch it had on the lower parts of the city, especially during the sticky summer months. The tram continues to wind up little streets with their overhanging cats' cradles of electricty cables, at one point passing the 1879 white multiturreted

STREETCAR THEATRE

Everyone on board the *bondinho* that shuffles its way up Santa Teresa is supposed to pay. But stand on the boarding ramp and the ticket collector will pretend you're not there and you travel free. When the train arrives at a station, all the 'rampers' jump off and stand around innocently whistling until the train starts to move, and they jump on again. In Rio de Janeiro this is known as *jeitinho* or getting away with it.

Below: *Mosaic stairway to a magical bohemia.*

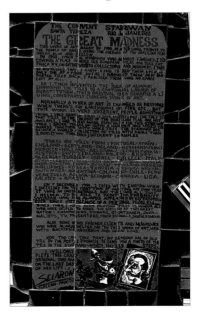

STREETCAR NAMED DESIRE

Fresh water was always a problem in Rio. Drinking wells or *chafarizes* had to be constructed. The nearest river was the **Rio Carioca** and to bring it in in sufficient quantities for the city's 16 fountains the **Aqueduto dos Arcos** (Arches of Lapa) was constructed. This high white aqueduct with its 42 arches, a feature of the city, ceased to be the city's water carrier in 1896 when the *bondinho* railway track was laid.

LIZARDS

The *tupinambis nigropunctatus* or tegu is a large black lizard with yellow spots. It is fond of chicken eggs but will gladly snack on other lizards, frogs and insects. They are not afraid of humans and sometimes lay their eggs 4m (13ft) up a tree in a termites' nest; the termites inadvertently protect them by enclosing them in their earthen carapace.

CASTLE ON THE HILL

Beau Geste fort or Bavarian dream, the **Centro Educacional Anísio Teixeira School** bearing up against a verdant Santa Teresa bluff is a crusader castle mirage. Crenellated battlements, lookout tower, ramparts and spindly palms. Preserved by the Office of State Patrimony, it is exotic and eclectic.

Bavarian-castle residence of **Fernando Valentim do Nascimento** (no relation to the artist Mestre Valentim of an earlier century). It looks like a wedding cake. Halfway up, the **Largo do Guimarães** is a major *bloco* (gathering point) for street carnaval bands. It is also a favourite place to dawdle, drink *chopp* and curse the government, and is generally known as Bohemian Santa Teresa. The line splits, one trundling onto **Neves Square**, the other to **França Square**. During the last weekend in May and November, the neighbourhood **Viva Santa** movement organizes a festival in which artists open the doors of their houses to visitors keen to buy works of art and local crafts. The **Museu do Bonde**, illustrating the history of Rio's streetcars is at 14 Rua Carlos Brandt.

There are three unusual places of worship in Santa Teresa: the **Russian Orthodox Church of Santa Zinaida** with its blue-onion domes in the Rua Monte Alegre, the **Anglican Cathedral of Saint Paul the Apostle** in Rua Pascoal Carlos Magno and the **Buddhist Temple** at Estrada Dom Joaquim Mamede, the only orthodox sixth-century Theravada centre in all of South America. Visitors are welcome to each.

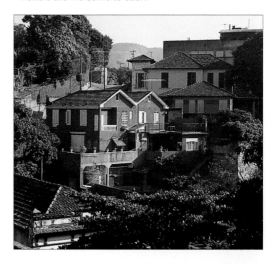

TAKE YOUR PARTNERS

In the early 19th century the old **Parque das Ruinas** house in Rua Murtinho Nobre was the place to be seen in high society. The owner **Laurinda Santos Lobo** converted her home into a fabulous *belle-époque* ballroom. It fell into ruin but was rebuilt in 1997 – the modern construction cleverly incorporating the old ruins and their evocative flavour of yesteryear. It is a great viewsite of Rio and Guanabara Bay.

Chopp and Snack ★★

Santa Teresa is a rabbit warren of quaint houses and little bars and restaurants. Try the **Bar do Mineiro** in Rua Paschoal Carlos Magno not far from Largo do Guimãres. The owner, an art collector, is known for his *feijoada* (*see* page 28). Or the *chopp* and pizza parlour at Largo do Curvelo, 6 Almirante Alexandrino with its blue and red interior. Meals arrive in a little lift from somewhere below and the two-storey restaurant looks down on Indian almond, prickly pear, guava, mango and breadfruit trees. In this same section of the street (keep an eye open for the trams going back and forth) is the handicraft shop, **La Vereda**. Ceramics, tapestries, paintings and furniture made from *madeira de lei* wood rescued from renovated colonial houses. The trams wander all over Santa Teresa's hillside. One way to explore is to walk part of the way back to town down Rua Almirante Alexandrino, branching off left and right as the fancy takes you. As always it's best not to be alone. A night tour by taxi is also fun.

In bygone days the haunting beat of African *macumba* drums would sometimes echo from Santa Teresa's forests, fires twinkling, as runaway slaves gathered to dance and plan revolt. And Cariocas would shiver in their beds.

MAN OF LETTERS AND ACTION

Benjamin Constant Botelho de Magalhães (long names are a feature of Brazilian nomenclature) was a man for all seasons. Politician, academic, engineer and military man, he was instrumental in bringing about the change from colonial empire to republic in 1889. He lived and died (1837–91) in Santa Teresa in what is now the museum named after him in Rua Monte Alegre.

5
Copacabana

Copa, as it is affectionately known, is a 4.5km (3-mile) scimitar of silver sand hugging a wide black and white mosaic promenade. With its yellow taxis, strolling dog owners, bicycles, *suco* kiosks and packed beachfront hotels it is probably the world's most famous playground. It is flanked at the rear by sheer granite slabs, coconut trees and jungle, and at the front by the blue Atlantic.

Early morning, before the six lanes (closed on Sundays) of buses and traffic hype into gear and as Sugar Loaf across the bay is still swathed in sea mist, is the best people-watching time. The whole of Rio seems to emerge to jog and dog-walk. Skate-boarders weave in and out of the walkman couples, the bikini beautiful, the sartorially daring and the *chopp* beer bellies. Every colour, every shape, every age can be seen on the wavy mosaic of Portuguese stone. Sit at one of the kiosks that sell ice-cold coco water, Carmen Miranda straw provided, and gawp. Here a lady in Ghanaian wraparound and Amazon headdress, there an iron-pumper in boutique trainers. Out at sea the first surfers and fishermen set off, while beneath an Indian almond tree a beggar taps with his white cane and when rewarded, walks off whistling, not blind at all.

Potted Palms, Diamonds and Fishing Nets ***
Interspersed among the 1930's Art-Deco hotels with their world flags, concierges, parking valets and potted palms, are innumerable restaurants, some boasting a hundred

DON'T MISS

*** **Copacabana Promenade:** the best beach stroll in Rio.
*** **Copacabana Fort:** Brazilian military history, Lovely views. Restaurant.
** **Copacabana Palace Hotel:** breakfast in elegance and luxury.
** **A-kilo restaurant:** pay by weight.
** **Swim** in the surf at sunrise.
* **Fishing kiosks and chapel:** near the fort and flotilla of surfers.
* **Júlio de Norona Square:** sculpture on Leme beachfront.

Opposite: *Copa's gleaming beach and holiday hotels from the air.*

Below: *Samba time on Copacabana beach.*

tables spread wide beneath canvas awnings across the pavement: Italian, Chinese, French, Russian, Indian and, of course, Brazilian. More American English is spoken on the Copacabana (or more accurately the promenade of **Av Atlântica**) than elsewhere in Rio. You'll find chic shops selling gemstones of which Brazil is a major exporter, and in Cassino Âtlantico's antiques mall everything a gold-carder could wish: coiffeurs, coffee shops, diamonds, Persian rugs, chinoiserie, and lawyers' offices. Before the 1946 prohibition, it was actually a casino. Now punters have to put up with the bingo parlour round the corner. In the same southern corner of Av Atlântica is the tiny beach chapel of Saint Peter where mothers pray that their fishermen sons will return from the sea. Boats and a fish market are also there and mid-morning you might even be able to buy an octopus. Soon the city wakes and it's time for exercises, beach football, fishing and streams of commuter cars heading for Centro.

Part male, Part female, Part fish ★★★

Long before the days of highway tunnels and population explosions Copacabana was a quiet sweep of pristine sand, mangroves and seabirds, inhabited by a small group of Tamoio Indians, the **Sacopenapá** (the word means a flamingo-like bird). Copacabana is actually named after **Cópac Awana**, a Bolivian Quichua god (and mountain city), part male, part female and part fish. Not unlike Demark's famous mermaid, Cópac Awana sat on a rock, but this time overlooking **Lake Titicaca**. God of the Seas, it was prayed to for an abundance of fish. Four hundred years ago a statue with Indian features swept up on Copa Beach was discovered by fishermen who named it **Nossa Senhora de Copacabana** (Our Lady of Copacabana). And soon the Virgin and the Bolivian god became one. In 1746 Bishop D Frei Antônio, spared from a terrible storm at sea off Copacabana, kept his promise and built a church in honour of the Virgin there. Today the church has been replaced by **Copacabana Fort** (*see* page 54) but the statue

Copacabana and Leme

is still revered in the nearby **Church of the Resurrection** in Rua Francisco Otaviano. Copacabana's patroness is remembered, if only tangentially, on 31 December each year with a candle-lit Candomblé procession from Madureira in the North Zone to Copacabana Beach, celebrating the feast and image of **Yemanjá**, Queen of the Sea.

Take the High Road *

Back from Av Atlântica the action gets even more exciting. Squeezed between sea and mountains, Copacabana is densely populated and this you'll soon see if you walk down **Av Nossa Senhora de Copacabana**. Internet cafés, shops, supermarkets, bookstores, laundries, bakeries and restaurants, dozens of chemists or *drogarios* (some 600 in Rio plus another 70 homeopathic pharmacies), *suco* fruit-juice stands, the Roxy cinema complex (get there early at weekends), and at No. 749, even a branch of the British clothes store C&A. Every two weeks free copies of *Posto Seis*, the Copacabana shopping tabloid (named after Copa's No. 6 beach guard post) are available in shops.

Copa's village and beach were really only reached by tracks until 1892 when the tunnel from Botafogo, now known as **Túnel Velho** underneath São João Mount, was constructed. **Túnel Novo** to Leme, the easternmost point

GENIUS OF FORM

Oscar Niemeyer was a prolific and imaginative architect. His influence is all over Rio. One unusual building in Copa is the pyramid of yellow waves against blue glass defining the **SESC** building (1995) in Rua Domingos Ferreira.

DEVIL ROCK

The long, traffic filled Avenida Nossa Senhora de Copacabana used to be blocked by hills known to the local Tamoio Indians as the 'stone of the devil' after the highest one. They were successively levelled by dynamite to make way for one of the world's busiest shopping streets.

Above: *Leme Bluff marks the easternmost sweep of Copacabana beach.*

of Copa, was opened in 1906, the year Av Atlântica was built. Being mountainous, Rio has many road tunnels including the 3km (2-mile) tunnel under the huge Tijuca urban forest. In 1923 came the **Copacabana Palace**, and rapidly thereafter Copa's international reputation as a tourism haven. Lack of land, meanwhile, in the interior of Brazil, and consequent susceptibility to shifting economic change, resulted in a massive influx of poor people into Rio, and the construction of hillside homes known as *favelas*. But in spite of this everyone wanted to live in exciting decadent Copa, particularly after the bossa nova boom of the 1950s. The much sought after Zona Sul increased in population by 1500% in the 50 years between 1920 and 1970.

Copacabana Fort **

Before Copa becomes Arpoador a crusader arch marks the entrance to Copacabana Fort, museum and modern military barracks. A lovely avenue of flowering trees and old artillery pieces lines the cobbled path dividing the red-tiled barracks from the sea wall. It leads to a circular 12m (40ft) thick underground fort built between 1914 and 1918 on the site of the old Nossa Senhora Chapel. Deep down, you walk through tunnels, batteries, past Krupp canons, engine rooms and 'bathrooms for lower ranks'.

On top of the fort as it hulks down on Arpoador Promontory the views of Copacabana and the tiny surfing beaches leading to Ipanema are magnificent. In the modern section there is a small but beautifully displayed military museum. A room-wide sculpted and painted fresco of the first Portuguese meeting Brazilian Indians on the shores of Brazil 500 years ago, marks the entrance. The displays include uniforms, helmets, swords, and life-size soldiers in historical battle scenes, even one of G.I's storming Italy's Monte Casino in World War II. On 5 July 1922, 32 soldiers from the fort rebelled against the government and 18 of them fought a pitched battle on Avenida Atlântica. Most were killed. Rio loves romantic heroes and a towering monument to Lt Rua Siqueira Campos, who led the troops, marks the exact spot of their last stand, further down Av Atlântica.

You will see flag-raising ceremonies and helicopters landing on the fort. On Sundays you can even ride around it by bicycle. Visit the curio shop and have coffee in the restaurant overlooking Copa Bay.

LEME *

Much as neighbouring Ipanema Beach is one with Leblon Beach so Copacabana is one with Leme – in effect, two vast beaches separated only by Arpoador Promontory. Both *bairros* (neighbourhoods) have some three to seven streets or blocks separating them from the *favelas* that cling precariously to Cantagalo, Cabrites, São João and Babilônia's granite hillsides, a process of urban sprawl that started 90 years ago. Leme occupies the northeast third of Copa. It's famous neighbour, Sugar Loaf, looms over its beach and jostle of esplanade hotels. It was a fishing village long before Copacabana.

Lying at the foot of the 210m (693ft) **Leme Bluff** with its granite cliffs and whispy palms, Leme's community is more tight knit than that of Copacabana, even cosy. It preserves a hunk of Rio's dwindling Atlantic rainforest on its heights. There's a path at its base to facilitate local fishermen, while on its peak is a flag marking the remains of the 230-year-old **Vigia Fort**, now a military reference centre. The view at sunset is magnificent. Just where the Fisherman's Walk begins is a lovely sculpture by **Angelo Venosa** locked at pavement level in the blue and white mosaic of **Júlio de Noronha Square**. It looks like a dinosaur's skeleton frozen in ice.

SIGHTS AND SOUNDS OF COPA

• The **Surf and Tattoo Gallery** at 67 Francisco Otaviano Street.
• Samba at **Bip Bop** on Tuesdays and Sundays at 50 Almirante Gonçalves Street.
• **Roxy Cinema**, Nossa Senhora de Copacabana 945, built in 1937. All claret and gold.
• **Morro dos Cabritos** still retains its pristine rainforest vegetation and affords a grand view of Copa.
• **Centro Comercial de Copacabana** shopping mall. Heart of Copa. Ritz gallery.
• **Av Rainha Elizabeth** off Av Atlântica features a Sunday fruit and vegetable market, and near **Rua Xavier da Silveira** a nightly art fair.
• **New Year's Eve** on the Atlântica, lit up with fireworks, attracts thousands.

Below: *Forte Duque de Caxias (Forte de Leme).*

6
Ipanema

Look at that gorgeous girl. In her samba stride, throwing back her hair, seeing but not looking at you, elegant, determined, mysterious. The girl from Ipanema (pronounced *Eepanyehma*). In her youth and vitality, her fresh-faced beauty, she still sums up this lovely neighbourhood with its little sidewalk cafés, wickedly pretentious shops, seductive bars beneath the trees and its stunning beach and promenade. Ipanema, birthplace of the sensuous bossa nova, the new sound that turned samba on its head.

On one side of Arpoador Bluff and Copa Fort that divides Rio's two great esplanades, you can look east to Sugar Loaf as the sun rises in a dazzle of blinding light across the sea. On the other, reached via the **Parque Garota de Ipanema**, sit on the rocks and you will see the whole sweep of **Ipanema Beach** stretching all the way to **Dois Irmãos** (the two brothers) – entwined conical peaks punching at the sky.

Arpoador Promontory **

Arpoador means whale harpoon. Catching the swells as they sweep around the bluff, it is an excellent place to hang ten and watch the board surfers riding the waves just beneath you. Brazil's first surfing championship took place here in 1950. Lit up at night, as is the whole of Ipanema Beach, Arpoador has the distinction of being the birthplace in Brazil of the bikini. It overlooks sand, surf, islands and the bluest of seas. And, yes, bikini beauties.

DON'T MISS

*** **Posto Nove:** Lifesavers beach tower. Meeting point for Rio's glamorous youth.
** **Garota de Ipanema Restaurant:** where *The Girl from Ipanema* was composed in 1962.
** **Rua Farme de Amoedo:** bohemians, music, cafés and the gay community.
** **Ipanema Beach Promenade:** sip a coconut at a kiosk.
* **Leblon:** shopping and the Jardim de Alah.
* **Hippie market:** Ipanema on Sundays.

Opposite: *The famous Ipanema Beach. Bold, brassy and beautiful.*

HIPPIE MARKET

The **Feira Hippie** is held on Sundays in the General Osório Square in Ipanema. Launched in 1969 by soul activist **Hugo Bidet** to help impoverished artists, it is popular with visitors but not quite Woodstock. The San Francisco beat generation of the 1960's were intellectuals, into Kerouac, jazz and red wine. Horrified by the free-love-marijuana-and-peace youngsters who imitated them, they labelled them with the diminutive put-down, hippie.

SAMBA KINDERGARTEN

The hilltop circular building in **Rua Alberto de Campos** looks like a spaceship. In fact it is a public school for 1200 pupils and a **Samba School Golfinhos da Guanabara** to help disadvantaged *favela* children.

The girl from Ipanema is featured all over Rio. The name of the bar where the song was written, **Garota de Ipanema**, is also the name of the tiny park and children's playground that gives access to Arpoador. It is a quiet place of flower sellers, palms, Indian almond trees, picnic tables, colourful murals and surfers loping through to the beach with their wickedly curved boards.

The Boys From Brazil *

Young folk of Ipanema are not shy about cuddling. It is never offensive or over the top, but you will see couples embracing at bus stops, in the street at traffic lights and of course on any park bench, of which there are several in **Praça General Osório**, a square built by Baron Ipanema in 1894. It occupies a whole city block on the corner of Rua Visconde de Pirajá – the Ipanema high street that links with Copa – and Rua Texeira de Melo. The fountain, topped by an obelisk and cross, was designed by **Mestre Valentim** in 1799. The so-called **Feira Hippie** craft market is held here on Sundays as it has been since 1969. Have a miniature iced *açaí* compote of this palm fruit mixed with Amazonian *guaraná* fruit, purple in colour, with granola sprinkle on the side. You eat it from a little cup with a spoon while you wander around.

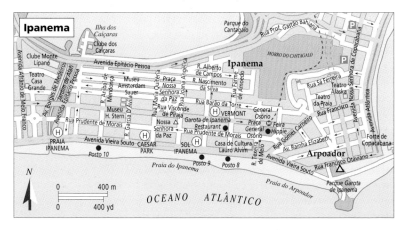

The general's square is the local gathering point for Carnaval *blocos* (bands). Banda de Ipanema parades are held on Saturday and Tuesday afternoons during Carnaval. It is popular with the gay and transvestite communities and was launched in 1965 in flamboyant protest against the then-dictatorship in Brazil. There are half a dozen

bands that gather in this vicinity, possibly the most outrageous being the **Banda da Carmen Miranda** in which gays dress up like the famous entertainer of the 1940s with her pineapple and fruit-salad headgear.

Above: *In Rio, the young and gorgeous will only be seen in what Cariocas call 'dental floss' bikinis.*

The great Bohemian meeting spot in Rio is **Rua Farme de Amoedo**, named after a 1917 city physician. Try a *cafézinho* (espresso), black and strong at the sidewalk **Cafeína** with its coffee-coloured décor.

Farme leads down to **Posto 8** on the beach where the rainbow flag flies. At night there is always music somewhere along this tree-lined street. In front of the more touristy restaurants are drums and samba, while street children do acrobatic flips between passing cars. Italian restaurants are a speciality, but **Bofetada Restaurant**, opened in 1937, still gets Brownie points for being popular with Girl from Ipanema co-writer, Vinícius de Moraes.

The Girl From Brazil *

The girl from Ipanema, the bossa nova song of 1962, put Rio on the world music map. Not since **Carmen Miranda** have so many tapped their feet and hummed a tune. It was composed by **Antônio Carlos (Tom) Jobim** and **Vinícius de Moraes** as they sat at their favourite bar, now the **Garota de Ipanema Restaurant**, in the street named after Vinícius de Moraes. Infatuated with schoolgirl **Heloisa** or **Helô Pinheiro** as she walked past daily, they were inspired. Originally sung by **Astrud Gilberto**, its English version stormed round the world. Rio's international airport is named **Antônio Carlos Jobim (Galeão)** or

THE GIRL FROM IPANEMA

High on an outside façade of Garota da Ipanema restaurant, in the original handwriting, are the words of the much loved song:
Tall and tan and young and lovely
The girl from Ipanema goes walking
And when she passes, …
… she's like a samba that
Swings so cool and sways so gentle …
Oh, but I watch her so sadly
How can I tell her I love her?
Yes, I would give my heart gladly
But each day when she walks to the sea
She looks straight ahead not at me …

Right: *Garota de Ipanema, the restaurant where* The Girl From Ipanema *was composed.* **Opposite:** *Surfing is Living. Only TV soaps beat surfing in Rio de Janeiro.*

just Tom Jobim, and there are seven Garota restaurants around Rio. To this day the girls of Ipanema like to think of themselves as that special 'tall and tan and young and lovely' girl from Ipanema. The first lady of Ipanema, however, was possibly the generous **Lauro Alvim** who donated her exquisite 1909 mansion to the neighbourhood as a cultural centre. It is on the **Avenida Vieira Souto** on Ipanema's promenade not far from **Barril's Bar** which is renowned for its super-chilled beer. The original Garota, formally named **Velosa,** is a wood-and-glass verandahed bar with blue roof tiles, pot plants and busy waiters. Popular with visitors, its prices have nudged upwards from the old Bohemian days 45 years ago.

Boutiques, Boulevards and Baseball Bats *

Ipanema is the fashion and boutique shopping mecca of Rio. The streets glitter with chic English and French names. Gringos (or foreigners – it is not an offensive word although *camarão* or lobster, is) are naturally attracted to it. You can shop for precious stones or just tour the workshops and sparkling exhibits in the Amsterdam Sauer and H. Stern jewellery museums. They are near each other in Rua Garcia D'Ávila. For music try Toca do Vinícius. The museum upstairs is all about bossa nova and Vinícius, the Ipanema Girl songwriter. Have a croissant from the Padaria de Ipanema (a bakery in Rua Visconde de Pirajá) or pause at Nossa Senhora da Paz's shady square, right in the middle of

Ipanema with its flower stalls, books and crafts. Ipanema officially ends just before the **Jardim de Alah** at the end of Av Visconde de Pirajá. The trams used to turn around here at **Alcazar de Toledo Square**, which is actually round and is today a frantic hurtle of traffic beneath an overhead walkway. It was built in the architecturally challenged 1950s and has a monument resembling a baseball bat.

Roasted Peanuts **

On Ipanema Beach, life is perfect. Good waves, lovely sand, plenty of sports, enough frozen coco juice kiosks to while away hours and exceptionally clean after-swim *postos*, the numbered shower units and loos maintained by the *prefeitura* (municipality). If you're a local, of course you may prefer to carry your board on sandy feet round to the waterfalls of Tijuca near lake Rodrigo de Freitas inland from Ipanema Beach. A long walk.

Sipping a kiosk coconut is a must on Ipanema Promenade. Here, a shy young lady from Chile will pass by with her display board of sharktooth earrings, or a man with Angolan features will place a little square of roasted peanuts in front of you. Just to taste, he says. Naturally you buy one of his cornets as he waits, wanting to know where you are from. He, of course, lives in the poor, 10,000-strong hillside *favela* of Cantagalo – named perhaps after its noisy roosters and strident music – that overlooks both Ipanema and Copacobana. Possibly he is a descendant of migrants who fled from Minas Gerais, the province adjacent to Rio, when gold mining collapsed (1920–30).

SEX AND THE CITY

Cariocas are ethnically and culturally mixed and this is reflected in their attitude to dress and sex. They don't approve of topless bathing, but they dress to attract. Every woman seems to be moulded into her Levi's, while men, usually in shorts, slops and T-shirts, will go shopping in a swimming costume. Sexuality, of course, has always played a major role in every culture. But sex, Cariocas would say, is not for hang-ups. Thus Rio caters for every taste, accepted or illegal, from the high-booted hooker hitching a ride on Av Atlântica, to the gays' rainbow flag on Ipanema Beach.

ACTORS AND ACTIVISTS

The **Casa Grande Theatre** in Leblon's Av Afrânio de Melo Franco has always combined opposition to military dictators, and pure theatre. Artists, liberals, poets and playwrights flocked to its banner and even risked their lives to raise funds for the incarcerated, plead for the persecuted and condemn injustices.

HIGHRISE WITH SOUL

Sundays feature an antique market at the eight-sided skyscraper in Leblon called the **Rio Design Center**, where the best of modern interior design in works of art, textiles, jewellery, lighting and furniture is on display.

Below: *Posto Nove's lifesaver tower is where Ipanema's youth frolic.*

Posto Nove **

Early in the morning you will see a lone labourer pull a huge trolley of deck chairs and umbrellas onto the beach. Soon the joggers and cyclists pour forth. There's a special lane for them. The kiosk on the promenade where Rua Garcia d'Ávila meets the sea is called **Barraca do Pelé**. Pelé himself has been renting out parasols, frescoballs and cellphones, and making sandwiches for his 4000 membership subscribers these past 25 years.

The section of the promenade called Posto Nove thinks of itself as young and cool. You'll see folk playing or being taught volleyball, futvolley (feet, chest and head only) and even the rather cruelly named vovôball after the floppy bellies of those who will never have a washboard tummy again.

LEBLON **

Leblon, a terribly smart suburb and continuation of Ipanema Beach, was named after Frenchman **Charles Le Blond** who had a pioneering fishing concern here in this land of sandbanks and mangroves in 1836. **Clipper**, the unofficial drinking hole of Rio soccer fans in Rua Carlos Góis, is a corner *botequim* or tavern (there are three in Leblon), where 'Leblon began to be Leblon'. It serves a superb draft *chopp* to its myriad sidewalk fans. On the promenade of **Delfim Moreira**, the Leblon half of Ipanema's curve of golden sand, is a children's play area in front of the beach, known as **Baixo Bebê**. It has toys, educational activities, birthday parties and stand-up tables for changing nappies. The **Beit Lubavitch Jewish Cultural Center and Synagogue** is a block down on Rua General Venâncio Flores.

There are some good bookstores in Leblon. **Livraria 2 Andares** on Rua Dias Ferreira

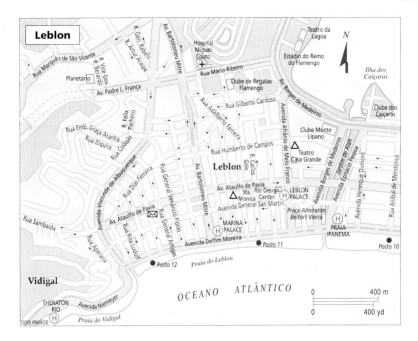

Ferreira sells English books (as do others in the area). It also boasts a café, **Severino**. There are actually cafés, bars and restaurants all over Leblon, some of which are open 24 hours. Leblon is known as the suburb between the canals namely **Jardim de Alah** and **Canal da Avenida Visconde de Albuquerque**. Both used to drain the waters of Lagoa Rodrigo de Freitas and divert the waters from Corcovado Mountain into the sea. Unfortunately the crabs and shrimps have long gone from the narrow cement channels.

Overlooking Leblon is the leafy suburb of **Alto Leblon**, with its big houses and swimming pools. Nearer to the sea and right up against **Dois Irmãos** is the pretty, protected **Parque Dois Irmãos**, formerly a coffee farm called Chácara do Céu. The nearby high-density *favela* goes by the same name. The park has a seven-level clifftop viewing area of the whole of Leblon and Ipanema.

URBAN GREEN LUNG

A dog guarding a child is one of several small statues in the **Jardim de Alah**, not Garden of Eden but named after the 1930s hit film starring **Marlene Dietrich**. It is a narrow sectioned park along both banks of the waterway linking the vast Rodrigo de Freitas Lake and Ipanema Beach. Jardim Botânico on the other side of the lagoon used to be one of Rio's slave markets. In Empire days, slaves were brought to it by boat, using the waterway. Today the garden is a favourite with dog lovers and nannies with children.

7
Garden and Lake

Growing in the wild all over the world are 25,000 species of orchids – those exotically beautiful flowers whose generic Latin name is *Orchideae*. Sixty thousand more artificial hybrids have been created by enthusiastic horticulturalists, a process that was invented in 1856. The 137ha (339-acre) **Jardim Botânico** (Botanical Gardens), near **Lagoa Rodrigo de Freitas** above Leblon, has a beautiful new orchid greenhouse of white columns, steel and glass.

JARDIM BOTÂNICO
In 1808, Rio's newly arrived Portuguese royal family expropriated the sugar plantation and mill of the De Freitas family (the area had grown sugar cane from early colonization days) and constructed **Casa dos Pilões**, the first gunpowder factory in Brazil. The mortar mill, an archaeological site and a museum in the gardens are all that remain of that often dangerous factory.

The administrator of the factory started a garden, which the emperor, who liked strolling, adopted, importing plants from all over Portugal's colonial world including India, China, French Guiana and Africa. Even the huge water lilies of Île de France (Mauritius) in the Indian Ocean were sent to Rio by Portuguese seamen captured by the French. All these and more can be seen in the gardens – 5000 trees and a total of 8500 different plants.

There are thousands of tropical palm species in Brazil. One, the *palmito*, is cut down for its delicious heart of palm used in millionaire's salad. Some of the most

DON'T MISS

*** Imperial Palms: great avenues of soaring palms in Jardim Botânico
*** Lagoa Rodrigo de Freitas Lagoon Walkabout: ski spray, mountains, mangroves and bird life.
** Lago Frei Leandro, Jardim Botânico: giant water lilies, palms and toucans.
* Eva Klabin Rapaport's private home museum: antiques and works of art.
* Mestre Valentim Memorial, Jardim Botânico: the great 18th-century Rio sculptor and artist.

Opposite: *Royal water lillies in Jardim Botânico's beautiful lake.*

THE MIGHTY PALM

There are raffia palms, royal palms, *açaí* palms and coconut palms among 1200 species in Brazil. They have been used by man for making rope, roofing and clothing, for food (e.g. *dendã* oil from Bahia) and for alcohol, such as toddy from the coconut palm. There is even one in Brazil with a bright orange heart. The world's tallest palm is the imperial palm and the largest palm nut is the 18kg (40lb) coco de mer of Seychelles.

impressive palms in the gardens are two great avenues of imperial or royal palms (*Roystonea oleracea*) from Central America. The palms stand 30m (100ft) high, soaring like sentinels, almost obscuring Tijuca Forest and the *Redentor* high above the park. The original palm planted by the king was destroyed by lightning in 1972.

Walking in the Park ★★★

Charles Darwin, during his great theory-of-evolution travels visited the Jardim Botânico in 1832. He would have reached them by canoe or by trekking along swampy trails. Today the bus drops you outside the entrance in the appropriately named Rua Jardim Botânico. They say up to 400,000 people visit the garden each year, but on weekdays, were it not for the well laid out paths, you could be lost on your own in a tropical forest, far from the bustle of Rio.

Highlights of a morning's stroll could include the Japanese Garden near the entrance gate and the Amazon Area next to it. Continue on the Aléia Karl Glass pathway and you'll come to the extensive rose

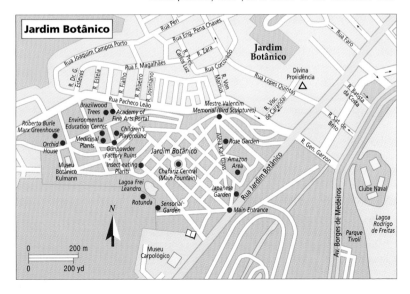

gardens. Nearby are the long-legged *pernaltas* bird sculptures at the Mestre Valentim Memorial, the first sculpture in bronze to be crafted in Brazil. The theme is the Greek myth about Echo, a lovesick nymph who was spurned by Narcissus (he who was so enamoured of his reflection that he turned into a flower) causing her to pine away until only her voice remained.

Nearby is the gardens' main fountain. The ornate and multi-faceted **Chafariz Central** was cast in iron in England in the late 19th century. Continue through various world forest types until you reach the rather intrusive buildings on Rua Pacheco Leão.

Brazilwood *

Follow the canal, **Rio Dos Macacos**, then head towards the **Rua Pacheco Leão** and you'll come to some of the very few remaining examples of the giant endangered **pau-Brasil** tree after which the country is named and which the earlier settlers 500 years ago exploited for its red dye. In the process they decimated much of the Atlantic rainforest. This phalanx of pau-Brasil leads to a rather grand Grecian portal – all that remains of the 1826 **Academy of Fine Arts**. Pause at the gunpowder factory ruins, children's playground, environmental education centre and the reserve for medicinal plants and herbs: 350,000 from all over the world.

The **Roberto Burle Marx Greenhouse** (he was a landscaping wizard) contains a variety of the wealth of brumelias that flourish in Brazil, many of which have found their way to other parts of the world

Above: *Like a phalanx of Trojan warriors, imperial palms salute the skies.*

TREE WALKING

The royal palm (*Roystonia regia*) grows gracefully upwards reaching a height of 30m (100ft). When Emperor Dom João planted the first trees in the Botanical Gardens, these palms were jealously guarded to preserve a monopoly on their cultivation. To little avail: agile slaves would 'walk' up the trees at night to steal the seednuts and sell them.

Capuchins and Toucans **

From the corner of the gardens where the Orchid House and attractive Administration House are located, make your way down to the **Lago Frei Leandro**, a lake built apparently by slaves under the supervision of Friar Leandro do Sacramento, the first director of the Botanical Gardens. Its Queen Victoria water lilies, looking for all the world like giant green pizzas, originally came from Mauritius. The elevated lookout **rotunda** was a favourite picnic site of both 19th-century emperors. If you are lucky you'll see capuchin monkeys (their heads resemble the hairstyles of Capuchin monks) and huge, gorgeously coloured toucans in the dense surrounding trees. The **greenhouse** of insect-eating plants includes pitcher plants whose tendrils look like Greek urns with lids. Along comes an unsuspecting ant attracted by the plant's sugary secretions, slips down the smooth side of the cup, the lid snaps shut and the pitcher has his snack for the day. Pitchers are usually of Asian origin.

Back to the main entrance you pass a delightful little waterfall before coming to the Sensorial Garden. This area of rosemary, basil, mint, jasmine, cloves and many others is designed for smell and touch by visually impaired people and the descriptive labels are in braille.

Where the Our Lady of the Holy Conception Sugar Mill was sited in the 16th century is the outdoor **Café Botânica** with wooden chairs and trees, Visitors' Centre, gifts and a bookshop. Walk past breadfruit trees along **Aléia João Gomes** and you'll come to the **library** which contains 66,000 volumes on botany, flora and fauna. The **Botanical Museum** with its arched entrance walkway features displays on environmental research and protection.

Early morning is magical – the best time for **bird-watching**. There are 140 species of birds including 20 different hummingbirds with their iridescent plumage

---

CHICO MENDES

There is a modest plaque in the gardens for the 'Peoples of the Amazon' including rubber workers and indigenous Indians of the forest. **Chico Mendes** worked on a rubber plantation as a child. He was a trade-union leader and fought hard to arrest the deforestation of the Amazon, and instead create protected botanical reserves. He was murdered in 1988 at the age of 44 by those who opposed his gallant fight.

SCARLET WOMAN

Scarlet macaws lay their eggs in the hollows of trees. These gloriously multicoloured birds with long tails and parrot beaks can be seen in Rio's Botanical Garden. They use their bills to climb along branches searching for the many fruits and nuts that form their diet. They like to congregate in groups in trees from where they watch you and even imitate your voice.

and vibrating wings. With luck you'll hear the even more colourful green-headed tanager songbird.

The Jardim Botânico is also a suburb, referred to rather oddly as **Suvaco do Cristo** (Christ's armpit) because it sits in the lea of the Tijuca Forest right under the southern arm of the outstretched Christ the Redeemer Statue atop Corcovado.

LAGOA RODRIGO DE FREITAS **

The lagoon called **Lagoa Rodrigo de Freitas** is surrounded by the suburbs of Ipanema, Leblon, and Jardim Botânico and in parts by mangroves. It attracts countless **birds** including the South American stilt, a mud-tip-toeing white bird similar to a heron and in some ways the flamingo. It was in honour of this bird that the Sacopenapã, a Tupi-Namba Indian group named the lagoon. They also called it, 'place of flat roots', referring no doubt to the mangroves. **Tom Jobim Park** surrounds two thirds of the lagoon and links up with several other parks including **Catacumba Park** near Copa. It is in effect a stretch of wooded lagoon shore with walkways, cycle track, sailing and rowing clubs. Catacumba boasts Rio's largest outdoor sculpture park.

The pathway flanking Av Epitácio Pessoa leads to **Chiko's Piano Bar** (renowned for good music), and the 1934 German Art Déco **Bar Lagoon** next door. It used to

> **TROPICAL LAND BUILDERS**
>
> Mangrove salt-water wetlands are rich in bird and marine life. The stilt-like roots of mangroves march forth in the mud, throwing out shoots and reclaiming land. The name comes from the Portuguese word *mangue* and in turn from an extinct Bahamas Indian Taino word. Tsunamis are less disasterous if coastal mangroves are not removed to create pristine tourist beaches.

Opposite: *A toucan takes five by the lakeside.*
Below: *Lagoa Rodrigo de Freitas from Tijuca forest.*

TONS OF TUNNELS

Túnel Rebouças which burrows under Corcovada Mountain linking Lagoa Rodrigo de Freitas and Rio's western suburb, is the longest urban tunnel in the world. Due to the existence of so many mountains in Rio, any cross-city trip will inevitably mean travelling through at least one tunnel.

Lagoa Rodrigo de Freitas

Rua Faro
Av. Borges de Medeiros
Jardim Botânico
São José da Lagoa
Parque Sacopenapá
Teatro F. Saudade
Rua Sacopã
Rua da Fonte da Saudade
R. Gen. Garzon
Ilha Piraque
Clube Naval
Lagoa Rodrigo de Freitas
Parque Tivoli
Av. Borges de Medeiros
Avenida Epitácio Pessoa
Parque Tom Jobim
Ponta de Pires
Parque da Catacumba
Parque Brig. Faria Lima
Hipódromo da Gávea
Avenida Epitácio Pessoa
Teatro da Lagoa
Estádio do Remo do Flamengo
N
Ilha dos Caiçaras
Parque do Cantagalo
Av. Borges de Medeiros
Clube dos Caiçaras
Clube Monte Lipano
Avenida Epitácio Pessoa
Jardim de Alah
0   400 m
0   400 yd

Below: *An imitation Mississippi paddle boat takes visitors to the Clube dos Caiçaras.*

be called Bar Berlin but was diplomatically renamed during World War II. The traffic on the one side of the walkway is a touch intrusive but the pretty girls learning to water-ski on the other compensate.

Caiçaras Island is actually a smart club, accessed by a blue and yellow imitation ferryboat, pert and manicured. There are lots of kiosks and street food vendors, paddle boats, palms and the occasional grizzled fisherman trying his luck.

Eva Klabin Rapaport's private museum in her former house on Av Epitácio Pessoa has some 2500 items: paintings, ceramics, oriental rugs and antique furniture. It is a gem. It is here that you have to cross the ferocious traffic to get to the **Jardim de Alah**.

Anyone for Tennis?

Flanking the western side of the lagoon there is a flotilla of aquatic clubs plus skating rink, equitation centres, tennis courts, soccer fields, a music amphitheatre and a heliport for trips above Rio. You can even learn the art of breadmaking at the **Escola do Pão** (School of Bread) in Rua General Garzon.

Old houses lie tucked away behind the skyscrapers and apartment blocks and some delicious little restaurants can be found along Rua Pacheco Leão flanking the Botanical Gardens in the Horto suburb. Bordering Atlantic forest, Horto supplies plants to the gardens. Also around Lagoa, in the neighbourhood named after Jardim Botânico, is the **Laje Park** which is situated right under Corcovado Mountain. Originally the home of ship-owner **Henrique Laje**, this old family palace, with its beautiful tropical gardens and grottoes, nearly went into complete decay when the owner died in 1940. It has since been saved by being declared a historical treasure. It houses the **School of Visual Arts**. The French restaurant of Claude Troisgros on the corner of Rua Custódio Serrão, with its yellow façade and cottagey ambience shaded by palms, is superb. And, of course, expensive.

The tiny limestone chapel, **Nossa Senhora da Cabeça** (Our Lady of the Head) is in Rua Faro. Built in the 17th century it is the last remaining rural or primitive chapel in Rio. It is situated in the grounds of an orphanage, **Casa Maternal Mello Matos**. There are some delightful waterfalls accessed via a footpath off Estrada Dona Castorina, while the best birds-eye view of the lagoon cupped by its enveloping mountains is off Rua Sara Vilela.

Above: *A South American egret, or garça, watches the water for supper.*

8
Tijuca

Tijuca is a vast range of forested mountains, ridges and peaks that form the backdrop to and infiltrate the whole of Rio, dividing the city into two: **Zona Sul** and **Zona Norte**. They flank the city from the outskirts of downtown **Centro** then south some 15km (9 miles) all the way to the seaside suburb of **Barra**, and inland another 5km (3 miles). In the north the range begins in **Tijuca** suburb itself, incorporates the 704m (2310ft) **Corcovado Peak** with the Statue of Christ the Redeemer, and finally ends at **Gávea** and the **Tijuca Lagoon**. Squeezed up against its awesome green mountains are the suburbs of Jardim Botânico, Leblon, Gávea, Vidigal, São Conrado and Lagoa Rodrigo de Freitas. It is the largest urban tropical forest park in the world. In spite of its luxuriance it is largely man-made, the original forest having been cut down for coffee growing. When the coffee began to starve Rio of its water supply in the mid-19th century, it was reforested over a period of 13 years. A 32km² (12-square-mile) national park of great beauty is Rio's inheritance today.

TIJUCA NATIONAL PARK

The **Tijuca National Park** is a lush mountain jungle of tiriba parrots, palms, waterfalls, Brazilian rosewoods, butterflies and silence. If you're a walker or mountaineer you can access Tijuca at any of a dozen trails from practically every suburb of Rio. The shortest route to the park is to take the Metro Line One to Saens Peña Station, then by road to Usina, onto Av Da Tijuca and

DON'T MISS

*** El Nido: sheer cliffs and isolated beaches.
*** Christ the Redeemer Statue on Corcovado: a train ride up takes 10 minutes.
*** Tijuca National Park Walk: Capuchin monkeys and cool quiet forests.
** Vista Chinese viewpoint, Tijuca: a pagoda vision of Rio crafted on rice paper.
** Museu International de Arte Naïf do Brasil: 8000 works of naïve art near the Corcovado cog train station.

Opposite: *Christ the Redeemer Statue stands 38m (125ft) high on top of Corcovado Peak.*

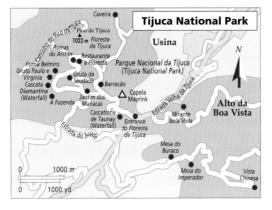

finally Estrada Velha da Tijuca to Afonso Viseu Square and the Alto da Boa Vista Heights. The stone gateway marking the entrance to the park leads to the Cascatinha path with its glistening waterfall and the pink and grey **Mayrink Chapel,** built in 1860. The **A Floresta** restaurant leads to the 1022m (3371ft) **Tijuca Peak**. On the way down, branch right and you will come to the grotto of Paulo e Virginia (named after the couple in the doomed Mauritian love-story). A small museum is along another pathway called the Estrada do Açude where, on Sundays, you can buy lunch and listen to the music.

Wild cats, sloths, capuchin monkeys and bats are some of Tijuca's mammals. Snakes include the famous boa constrictor and the many birds include woodpeckers and black-billed toucans.

Chinese Point of View **

Another route by car is up from Leblon to Rua Jardim Botânico and the Rua Lopes Quintas. This route will take you past the delightful **Vista Chinesa** overlooking Leblon. This pagoda lookout was named after indentured Chinese labourers who built roads in Tijuca Forest in the 19th century, and originally assisted Rio's ill-fated Chinese tea growing experiment. It was their camp site. The twin-storey open hexagon has dragon heads at each corner. Brazilian poet José de Alencar was moved to comment: 'The Vista Chinesa is an oriental vision crafted on rice paper of sublime delicacy.'

Several roads wind their way through view sites in the Carioca mountain range between Tijuca suburb and Lagoa Rodrigo de Freitas, while others link Alto da Boa Vista with Jardim Botânico, Corcovado and Gávea.

CORCOVADO PEAK
Rio's Redeemer ★★★

No matter where you are in Rio, by day or lit by greenish light at night, you can see the great statue of **O Cristo Redentor** (Christ the Redeemer) atop Corcovado Peak. The statue, 30m (100ft) high on its 8m (25ft) pedestal, was completed on 12 October 1931 by engineers **Heitor da Silva Costa** and **Pedro Viana**. Renowned French sculptor **Paul Landowski** made the head and hands. The statue is made of reinforced concrete and covered with millions of pale green triangular shaped, interlaced mosaics of soapstone which can be seen through binoculars. The statue is so huge that even when you walk to the furthest point of the view platform it is difficult to get it all in camera frame. Known by Cariocas as the *Cristo* or *Redentor* it seems to endlessly embrace Rio and its people, good and bad, young and old, rich or poor. Not that Cariocas are particularly ardent in their faith, but they are proud of their *Redentor*. The statue weighs 1145 tons – the head alone weighs 30 tons and the arms 88 tons each. The distance between the Christ's outstretched arms measures 28m (30yd). It was planned for Brazil's 100th centenary of independence from Portugal in 1922. The floodlighting was designed by the Italian radio inventor **Guglielmo Marconi** and with modern adjustments is still in use. It was he who turned the lights on 12 October 1931 by remote, all the way from Geneva, Switzerland.

Red Forest Train ★★★

There are several ways to get to Corcovado, the most exciting and easiest being the 10-minute journey by the **trem do Corcovado** (cog train) which you catch from the busy station at Rua Cosme Velho. Taxi drivers at the bottom, eager for a fare, will call out to you that the train has just gone, and

Below: *A redeeming embrace of Rio's Christ, the Son.*

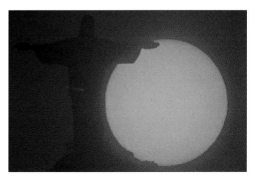

in fact if there are several of you, a taxi works out cheaper. You can also walk the 9km (5 miles) up the steep shady road, the entrance to which is at the right of the station. The train's route is just under 4km (2 miles) long and it snakes through forest, past the occasional bungalow and high over the winding road that also leads to the top. It operates every 20–30 minutes, 08:30–18:00. The railway was officially opened by **Emperor Dom Pedro II** in 1884 and the first trains were steam driven, to be replaced by electricity in 1910. Smart new Swiss-made trains came into service in 1979. You travel up slowly at 15kph (10mph), passing the occasional group of school children walking home on the tracks. Sit on the right for the best Tijuca mountain and forest views. The twin railway carriages carry 120 passengers and at Paineiras Station the train pauses to allow the one coming down, to pass.

From the upper terminus, lined with gleaming eco-friendly receptacles – one each for glass, paper, plastic and organic matter – it is a winding path of 220 steps to the top. There are at least two restaurants en route and more ubiquitous tourist shops, so stop if you're puffed. You can also go up in the new escalator. The view platform surrounding the *Redentor* is shaped like a huge tennis racquet. There are several explanatory plaques and a small chapel at the base. It is always fairly crowded but the views are mesmeric. There are no pay telescopes so bring binoculars if you want to study virtually the whole of Rio, ocean, mountain and city around you. Below you, the sunlight dances off patches of grey-white leaves on top of the forest canopy as the birds swirl and dive in the stiff breeze, while miles below and all around stretch the white matchbox suburbs of Rio.

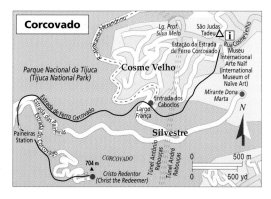

TIJUCA SUBURB

Tijuca suburb is an old district. Its Usina neighbourhood has the oldest high school in Rio, the handsome **Colégio Marista São José**, built in 1852 and taken over by the Marist Brothers 50 years later. **Bar da Dona Maria** is a famous 60-year-old boteco bar well known as a gathering place for soccer stars and samba. Tijuca also used to be the cinema centre of Rio.

The slogan of the Andarai district's **Salgueiro Samba Troupe** in Rua Silva Teles proudly proclaims that they are: 'no better, no worse, just different'. Salgueiro is in fact a poor hillside *favela* area but its samba school and patron saint Sebastian (the patron saint of Rio) have won honours in all but five of the 47 years it has participated in Carnaval.

Above: *Pagoda with a view, at Vista Chinesa.*

Cagebirds, a Rio obsession, are bought and sold on Sundays at the **Praça dos Passarinhas** with its large fountain and mosaic cobblestones.

The huge marshland around Tijuca Rainforest, incorporating today's Tijuca suburb, Maracanã Stadium, Quinta da Boa Vista and São Cristóvão all the way to Guanabara Bay, was originally developed for sugarcane by Jesuit priests. In 1567 they built Rio's first mill, **Engenho Velho**, and in 1583 a chapel dedicated to St Francis Xavier. Today's church with its white and grey twin towers, palms and cupolas, was built on the chapel site. Due to metro underground construction, its dome collapsed in 1960 and the church had to be rebuilt. The Jesuits clashed with the government and were expelled in 1759. Their estates were sold to small plot owners, who in turn were rapidly bought out by wealthy country cousins. The forests were decimated to make way for coffee. In 1859 the first donkey-pulled trams to be operated in South America went from Rio Centro up to Boa Vista. They were known as Tijuca-cars or *maxabombas*.

TIJUCA FOLK

The residents of Tijuca have always thought of themselves as simple country folk, as they have easy access to the forests and mountains that surround them. But not all Tijucans yearned for the great outdoors. **Joércio Samarão** and his wife **Hermesilia** fancied something a little grander. In 1914, world war or not, they built their three-storey cream coloured mansion in the suburb with materials imported from France: eclectic architecture with twirls and balustrades, stained-glass windows, an elevator indoors and a concrete eagle on the cupola.

9
Southern Coast

Gávea can be divided into three: the part near the Jockey Club and Hipódromo Da Gávea, then Alto da Gávea near the mountain park of Tijuca and Dois Irmãos, and finally Gávea by the sea. In 1502, sea captain **Gaspar Lemos** was one of several sailors to describe the 842m (2776ft) vertical rock between today's Leblon and Barra da Tijuca, as 'Gávea' or ship's mast and crow's nest. Today its neighbour, the 696m (2300ft) **Pedra Bonita**, is a sky-diving rock.

You can also access Barra da Tijuca by driving along the old twisting Estrada da Gávea, or through the Túnel Dois Irmãos from Av Padre Leonel Franca, the Lagoa–Barra Freeway that starts near the Jockey Club.

GÁVEA

Gávea is Rio's oldest suburb, having been occupied centuries ago by French colonists in search of Brazilwood. Sugar cane came next, then coffee. Until quite recently Gávea was a distant cousin of Rio, a rural suburb of farms and livestock, inhabited by landed gentry keen on splendid isolation. Then, in the 1880s, came the textile factories and everything changed. Gávea became so industrialized that during the 1918 General Strike it became known as 'Red Gávea'.

Streetcars were followed by roads, particularly over the mountain and the sea hugging Avenida Niemeyer, privately constructed by property magnate Commander Niemeyer in 1916. It was not until 1937 that Zona Sul was declared a non-industrial area.

DON'T MISS

*** Favela tour: the vibrant mountain-hugging suburbs of Rio's poor.
** Av das Américas, Barra da Tijuca: born in the USA.
** Barra da Tijuca beach: 22km (14 miles) of golden sands.
* History of Rio de Janeiro City Museum: Rio since 1567.
* Sinless Motel: look out for it along the sinuous Vidigal road in the shadow of Dois Irmãos peaks.
* Pepino Beach: where the hang gliders land.

Opposite: *Gávea's great granite obelisk stands guard over beach and sea.*

FRIENDS AND NEIGHBOURS

The word *favela* comes from the word stinging-nettle hill, so named by a platoon of soldiers 100 years ago, to describe the hill where they placed their artillery. Back in Rio the soldiers (now nick-named *favelados*) also built their homes on a hillside, and the word stuck. Great strides have been made and much money has been put into demarginalizing these hills of hunger and incorporating them into their neighbouring rich suburbs. There is rubbish collection, transport, street construction, sewerage, day-care centres, even a branch of McDonald's.

PEPINO'S BEACH

Good girls never went to **Praia do Pepino** in São Conrado in the 1940s. Its wild location and wild waves may have been conducive to fun but not to respectable reputations. The beach is the furthest end of Gávea Beach. The golden youth of Rio gathered there in later years while today its fabulous waves are sought after by surfers and its wide beach as a landing strip for hang-gliders.

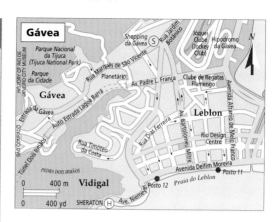

Sinless Lunches ★★

Vidigal, just beyond Leblon in the lea of Dois Irmãos, consists of a small beach that belongs to the Sheraton Towers Hotel, a *favela* visited by Pope John Paul II in 1980, and the exotic Sinless Motel. **Nós do Morro** (we of the hillsides) drama group in the *favela* is one of Rio's leading theatre companies. **Praia São Conrado** is a small portion of the larger **Praia de Gávea**. All roads, they say, meet in São Conrado, described by one writer as 'a refined address'. On **Pepino Beach** near the luxuriant **Gávea Golf Club,** whose first members were predominantly English and Canadian, you can watch the colourful hang-gliders land.

On the **Estrada da Gávea** (a little inland from the beach) is the **São Conrado 'Fashion Mall'** boasting chic boutiques, restaurants with foreign names and leafy walks. On the same *estrada* is the old 18th-century plantation house, **Vila Riso**. On 13 May 1888 (on a table which can still be seen in the Vila) the then Minister of Justice and owner of the house, Antônio Ferreira Viana, signed the *Lei Áurea* giving Brazilian slaves their freedom. On Sundays you can combine your visit with a good lunch that is served here.

Elevado das Bandeiras (also known as Elevado do Joá) curves sinuously above the rocky coast of São Conrado and Praia de Gávea, revealing a gorgeous view of surfers at the exquisite **Joatinga Beach**, with its exclusive **Costa Brava Club** perched on a tiny island offshore. It is accessed by a 90m (300ft) free-span bridge; a rewarding if precarious spot for weekend fishermen as well.

Gávea Heights *
Gávea Heights is an upmarket suburb like Alto Leblon. It lies south of Lagoa's **Jockey Club**. Since 1970 Gávea's forested streets and small-community atmosphere have been preserved by the banning of many new buildings and shopping malls. It is an expensive residential area with some good restaurants. The **Jequitibá National Heritage Tree** is in Rua Marquês de São Vicente.

Off the main Lagoa-Barra highway is the **Planetário** (planetarium) and the fly-over residential building of **Minhocão-Conjunto Residencial Marquês de São Vicente**, Rio's longest one-breath name. Nearby is the large campus of the Jesuit Catholic University, PUC-Rio, with its massive columned verandah, a favourite with film makers and student protestors.

The **History of Rio de Janeiro City Museum** is situated in the mountainous **Parque da Cidade** on an old coffee plantation of lakes, lawns and ocean views. Its 17,000 exhibit items relate the story of Rio's growth as a city since its beginnings in 1567, right through to 1950. Estrada da Gávea twists and turns past Rio's largest *favela*, **Rocinha**, and is an alternate route to the Dois Irmãos tunnel between Lagoa and Barra da Tijuca.

Left: *On the wings of the wind – hang gliding from Pedra Bonita.*

COUNTRY COUSINS

Gávea Golf and Country Club (*see* page 80) in São Conrado is English-named because it was started in the 1920s by a group of English and Canadian sportsmen. Its mountains, greens, fees and lush vegetation make it very country indeed. The clubhouse is known as the **Casa Azul** (Blue House) and was the original cane-crushing mill on this old estate. (At weekends, by member invitation, tel: 3322-4141.)

EYE OF TUCAN AND TOE OF BOA

Macumba is the old and not very nice word Cariocas use for all Afro-Brazilian religions. *Quibanda*, the correct word, basically means **voodoo**. It is rare today but it wasn't during slavery days. How else could one deal with an all-powerful slave master? **Praia da Macumba** between Recreio and Prainha in southern Barra was named after the black arts supposedly practised on the beach in the dead of night by slaves.

Opposite: *Rocinha* favela – *much more than meets the eye.*
Right: Favela *gals banter with passers-by below.*

Rocinha: Proud Favela ★★★

The wicked of the world say that all you have to do in Rocinha if you're looking for cocaine is to sit at one of the tiny pavement bars near the *boca* or mouth (it refers to the taking of the drug), call one of the waiting black leather-capped motorbike taxis and he'll roar up the steep winding street to purchase it for you. Don't even think of trying it: heavily armed cops will come after you and the consequences are dire.

Dois Irmãos looms over the poverty-stricken breeze-block houses on the slopes of Rocinha that divide the suburb of Gávea in two. It is a fascinating, noisy, crowded place of at least 200,000 people. Tiny alleyways, sewerage, wary cats and washing lines. It began in the 1920s. With so little land available to poorer folk in the countryside, people poured in to seek work and survival in the city. There are many *favelas* in Rio. This is the largest. It is something out of Charles Dickens' London. But ironically, in spite of being incorrectly labelled the world's largest urban slum (one perhaps needs to look to the plastic-and-tin shanties of Africa and India for that), Rocinha is a genuine and proud neighbourhood with a photo lab, banks, schools, sports centres, supermarkets and 2500 businesses – albeit often operating with an inadequate water supply and illuminated with stolen electricity.

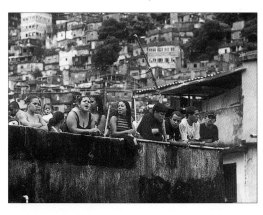

Favelas are not for the faint hearted. Only go in with a local. There are mean streets here, mean hillsides. But go on an organized tour and you will meet real people, hard-working people, with loves, sorrows, achievements and above all humour, in spite of grinding poverty. There's a small tourist office in Rocinha where community guides will take you on an hour's tour.

BARRA DA TIJUCA

South of Leblon and Gávea Beach is the **Barra da Tijuca** (often merely called Barra and pronounced *baha*). It lies between a flotilla of four huge lagoons and a 22km (14-mile) beach. It is Rio's favourite weekend retreat for volleyball, ski surfing, fishing, barbeques and picnics. Its wetlands used to be huge sugar-cane *fazendas* with access only on horseback or by boat. Barra became Rio's new neighbourhood in the mid-1960s and within 10 years the Lagoa–Barra Freeway and the Dois Irmãos Tunnel made it easy to reach. Towering sea-fronting luxury condominiums were soon being built, and there are some 160 of them today. None are particularly attractive, but all are self sufficient with shops, banks and schools. Av Sernambetiba runs the length of the beach, while Av das Américas with its rather odd proliferation of Arizona shopping malls (actually called 'shoppings') cuts through the suburb inland. Barra is Rio's richest suburb. Here you have the **New York City Center**, **Statue of Liberty**, **Hard Rock Café** and vast supermarkets such as **Carrefour**, **Extra Freeway**, **Barra**

FLY LIKE A BIRD

There are many companies and *rampas* (launch sites) atop granite peaks in Rio for piloted, tandem hang-gliding. **Pedra Bonita** in Gávea is one. They will pick you up and drop you off at your hotel or you can make arrangements on **Pepino Beach**. Know your exact weight in kilograms (ideally under 80kg), as adjustments to weight belts and size of glider will need to be made. You can even have pictures taken of yourself in flight.

BETWEEN A ROCK AND A HARD PLACE

The nimble waiters at the **Hard Rock Café** in Barra's Shopping Città América serve you while dancing to the non-stop beat of guitars and drums. You could be at a Republican election convention it is so American. Besides the restaurant there are bars, a nightclub and a shop. Rio's Café is the group's second largest in the world.

ISLAND IN THE SUN

There is only one street on the small **Ilha da Caroa** in the middle of the smallest of Tijuca's lagoons. You can walk across the small bridge or catch an informal ferryboat.

World Shopping (with replicas of the Eiffel Tower and readings of Shakespeare) and traffic jams to match. Barra World Shopping is the largest mall in South America with 540 shops and 25 million punters annually. The complex has 30 clinics while the New York City Center has 18 movie screens.

When you finally reach shop-to-drop exhaustion there's a nice park at the crossroads of Av das Américas and Av Ayrton Senna, the latter linking Barra to inland Jacarepaguá, and eventually all the way to North Rio. The fish market and fish restaurant in Av Ayrton Senna is worth a visit. The Marriot, Sheraton and Transamerica hotel chains are all here. International congresses are held in Barra at, for example, Riocentro whose five pavilions are linked by covered walkways, the whole surrounded by green hills, palms and water courses. The vast **Lagoa de Jacarepaguá** (meaning lagoon of alligators in Tupi-guarani) is visible from the top. You can buy a secluded bungalow beneath palms in the middle of one of the lagoons that frame Barra, but the lagoons are under pollution threat. The beach is lined with hundreds of kiosks selling iced beer, coconuts and *caipirinhas*.

Situated in the far western corner of Barra is the **Praia Recreo dos Bandeirantes**. It is basically an army of white condos drawn up in battle formation. But the nearby **Biological Wetland Reserve** and *restinga* (sandbar) makes

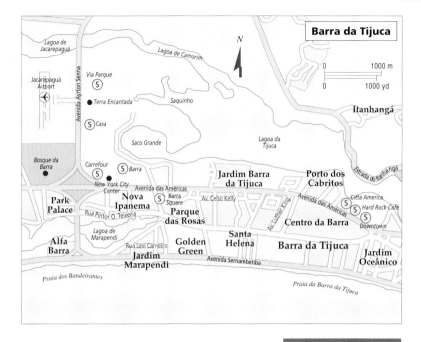

Barra da Tijuca

Lagoa de Jacarepaguá

Lagoa de Camorim

N

0   1000 m

0   1000 yd

Jacarepaguá Airport

Via Parque (S)

Terra Encantada

Saquinho

Itanhangá

(S) Casa

Saco Grande

Lagoa da Tijuca

Bosque da Barra

Carrefour   (S) Barra

New York City Center

Avenida das Américas

Jardim Barra da Tijuca

Porto dos Cabritos

Estrada do Itanhangá

Park Palace

Nova Ipanema

Rua Pintor O. Teixeira

(S) Barra Square

Av. Celso Kelly

Parque das Rosas

Cittá America

Av. Luiz Carlos King

Avenida das Américas

(S) Hard Rock Cafe

(S)

Centro da Barra

Downtown

Alfa Barra

Lagoa de Marapendi

Rua Levi Carneiro

Golden Green

Santa Helena

Barra da Tijuca

Jardim Oceânico

Jardim Marapendi

Avenida Sernambetiba

Praia dos Bandeirantes

Praia da Barra da Tijuca

up for it. The latter is a pristine stretch of beach and lagoon untouched by development. The **Chico Mendes Ecological Park** is just around the corner and the beaches at **Praia do Pontal Macumba** are very popular with surfers.

GONE FISHING

A multicoloured mosaic breakwater leads out into Barra Bay. **Quebra-mar**, built on great chunks of stone with a thatched kiosk on stilts halfway along, is a favourite with fishermen and surfers.

Opposite: *The lonely sea and the sky. And 160 condominiums at Barra's vast beach.*
Left: *A spaceship fishing platform near Barra attracts patient anglers.*

10
Flamengo, Glória and Catete

The open-air leisure park at Flamengo is a refreshing green oasis. The 100ha (247 acres) of trees, lawns, flowers, bandstands, children's playgrounds and pathways stretches over 4km (2 miles) – the length of the **Flamengo**, **Catete** and **Glória** suburbs that face blue Guanabara Bay.

Flamengo was once a marshy area of rivers on which flamingos pecked and preened when the first Portuguese arrived 500 years ago, saw these pink blushing birds and named them for the first time. It soon became a port to export the sugar of the distant Lagoa plantations where the **Engenho d'El Rey** (King's Cane Mill) had been built.

Flamengo has a bicycle track, tennis courts, model-aeroplane sites, eight soccer fields and puppet shows, a blessing for the children and residents who daily have to face the heavy through traffic of the area. Here youngsters learn soccer, fishermen try their luck, teenagers skateboard and their elders stroll and chat. The park with Sugar Loaf on the right as you face the bay was designed by world-renowned landscape designer **Burle Marx** on land reclaimed from the sea, using 1.2 million metric tons of rubble and earth. It was opened in 1965.

PARQUE DO FLAMENGO
Carmen's Magic ***
The circular **Museu Carmen Miranda** (in memory of Rio's greatest singer and theatrical personality) is at the southern end of **Parque do Flamengo** (Flamengo Park).

DON'T MISS

*** **Nossa Senhora da Glória do Outeiro:** ancient Royal Chapel of emperor's and kings sits by the sea.
** **Largo do Boticário Square:** cobblestones, old-world houses, leafy trees.
** **Palácio Laranjeiras, Guinle Gardens:** how the grandees lived.
** **Largo do Machado:** kiosks, fountains, flowers, bookstalls.
* **Museum of Modern Art:** on the seafront.
* **Carmen Miranda Museum:** pineapple queen of stage and film.

Opposite: *Flamengo Castle huddles in a twirly coven of high-rises.*

Above: *Pastel shades and sparkling lights over Flamengo as night falls.*

There are 3000 items on display including her gowns and jewellery and the video is particularly worth watching.

Nearby, surrounded by lawn and interspersed concrete circles, is the statue of **Cuauhtémoc** the Aztec emperor. The old 1895 **Flamengo Football Clubhouse** is also sited here. The 1916 ochre-coloured **Flamengo Castle** has a slate-tiled witches' tower and enough eclectic columns, Moorish balustrades and window nooks to suit any Romeo and his Juliet. President Getúlio Vargas committed suicide on 24 August 1954 on the third floor of the presidential **Palácio do Catete**, now the **Museu da República**. Finished in 1866, it used to be the home of coffee magnate, Barão de Nova Friburgo.

For the Children *

The park's construction was inspired by activist **Maria Carlota Macedo** who wanted a proper place for children to play. Today there is a fully staffed nursery. The beach is not suitable for swimming but a great place to watch sailboats heeling over in the wind, as they leave Glória Marina. The Marina is near Santos Dumont Airport, where flights to São Paulo shuttle regularly across Guanabara Bay. There is a sailing school, boatyards, navigation station and the main docking facility can accommodate yachts of up to 30m (100ft).

The World War II Memorial *

The World War II Memorial soars upwards as if offering the souls of the gallant dead to the Almighty. The remains of Brazilian soldiers killed in Italy (1944–45) are buried in the underground crypt, while the first floor is a war museum. Military parades are held here on the vast open surrounds.

MEA CULPA

The impressive **Church of Our Lady of Glória** in the tree-lined square of the same name is rich in small statues, paintings and religious *objets d'art* given to the church by its wealthy 19th-century parishioners, either out of genuine piety, to expiate their sins or, some would say, to flaunt their wealth. It was completed in 1872.

Museu de Arte Moderna **

The Museum of Modern Art with its machete-like flying buttresses is next door. Built in 1948, its collection was all but obliterated by fire in 1978, but has since recovered to offer 11,000 works of sculpture, painting, drawing and engraving, many donated by well-wishers abroad. The 19th-century photography exhibit is excellent and the museum, surrounded by palms and ponds, has a bookstore, design store and a restaurant. Its Cinematica trains Brazilian film-makers.

GLÓRIA
Glorious Church ***
Nossa Senhora da Glória do Outeiro (Our Lady of Glory of the Sacred Hill) was begun in 1714 but only completed 77 years later. Its bell tower with

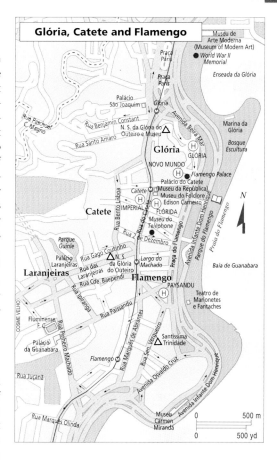

palms and banners flying proudly in the wind, overlooks the sea from its 60m (200ft) hilltop eyrie. Lit at night, it is still the most beautiful structure in Glória. Baroque polygonal in style (lots of angles and sides) it became the royal chapel when the Portuguese court fled from Napoleon to Brazil. Emperor Dom Pedro II was baptized here. Its main wooden altar is believed to have been carved by Rio's most famous sculptor **Mestre Valentim** and the interior reveals some of the most outstanding examples of Brazil's blue-faced tiling.

GEMS ON THE BAY

The half-moon balconies of **Edifício Biarritz** rise one upon the other like towering piles of delicate saucers. The Art-Deco building in **Praia do Flamengo** was designed in 1940. Also on Flamengo bayfront is the tall **Edifício Flamengo**, built 10 years earlier, this time with a busy Moorish theme. It was the darling of Rio when it was first constructed.

Before the glory days of Carnaval, the **Outeiro da Glória Festival** used to be the most widely attended in Rio: religious fervour, fireworks, music and feasting. The church is now separated from the sea by landfill, the new **Flamengo Park** and the white colossus of the luxurious old-world **Hotel Glória**, which in 1922 was the first reinforced-concrete construction in Rio. Today, with a judicious extension, it has 630 rooms and caters for heads of state. At one time such illustrious celebrities as Rudyard Kipling and Ava Gardner stayed there.

Templo da Humanidade *

The 19th-century philosopher **Auguste Comte** believed that experimental investigation and observation were the fount of knowledge. His positivist views became popular in Rio to the extent that a church (the only positivist one in the world) was built in 1897 along Rua Benjamin Constant in Glória. The positivist motto 'Order and Progress' is actually inscribed on Brazil's blue and yellow flag.

Praça Paris **

Praça Paris, part of the green Flamengo beltway and inspired by the Tuileries in Paris, is huge. As are its lakes and fountains and formal gardens. Not to mention its exotic bronze busts and marble statues exalting the glories of nature and its seasons.

Below: *Rua do Catete pedestrian mall on a Saturday morning.*

CATETE
Museu do Folclore Edison Carneiro *

The Museu do Folclore Edison Carneiro in the Rua do Catete is an 18th-century townhouse with exhibits not unlike those in that other wonderful folk-art museum Casa do Pontal, beyond Rio (*see* page 118). Ceramic folk figures depict every aspect of Brazilian life: villages, religious characters, Candomblé festivals.

Museu do Telephone *

The Telephone Museum in Dois de Dezembro takes the visitor back 120 years, covering the fascinating history of the telephone. There is a replica of Dom Pedro II's telephone and the gold one used by the popular president Gétulio Vargas, who shot himself in the heart in the Palácio do Catete in Glória in 1954 when the military tried to force him out of office.

Palácio do Catete **

The **Palácio do Catete** (1858) is made of stonework from France and further lavishly appointed with Parisian ironmongery. It was later to become the seat of the Brazilian Republic for 63 years. When Brazil's capital moved to Brazilia in 1960 however, the building became home to the **Museu da República**.

Largo do Machado **

The **Largo do Machado** was redesigned in 1954 by **Burl Marx**, master of landscaping. It was a marshland some 150 years ago. Today its trees, kiosks, fountain, flowers, bookstores and mosaic walkways face the **Church of Our Lady of Glória** (1834–72), not to be confused with the one on the hillside overlooking Guanabara Bay.

DAZZLING WHITE

The filigree iron grillwork surrounding the grounds of the Portuguese hospital in Rua Santo Amaro is intricate and elegant. The hospital was built in 1840. The fretted woodwork inside is supremely artistic and its many paintings on the walls trace the history of Portugal, a tiny nation that ruled the waves and a worldwide empire 500 years ago.

LEAVE ME NOT, MY LOVE

Iracema the 'virgin with the honeyed lips' is the heroine of Brazilian 19th-century writer **José de Alencar**'s novel. The novel portrays the Portuguese conquest of Brazil romanticized into a love story between a beautiful Indian woman and a brave colonist, Martim Soares. She dies in childbirth, but their mixed-race son, Moacir lives on. As does multicultural Brazil. A seated statue of Alencar can be seen in the square of the same name in Flamengo.

Above: *Cosme Velho's Largo do Boticário or Apothecary's Square is a gem of historic pastel-coloured homes.*

BACK OF THE BAY
Cosme Velho and Laranjeiras

The old **Cosme Velho** and **Laranjeiras** (oranges) neighbourhoods initially spread out along the **Carioca River**. It brought water from the surrounding hills and eventually flowed into Flamengo in two streams, one called **Catete**. Channelled first with wooden beams then with stone, the Carioca River was eventually covered over to flow underground. Before that it crossed the lovely arched **Lapa Aqueduct** and in 1723 provided water for the first water spring made of stone at **Largo da Carioca**. **Oscar Niemeyer**, the renowned architect, was born here, along Rua Cardoso in the district called 'Little Portugal'. In the late 19th century the Largo area was known for its busy tramlines and a huge textile factory.

The **Largo do Boticário** (Apothecary's Square) in Rua Cosme Velho is an exceptionally beautiful little 19th-century gem that goes back to 1831, with homes painted in pastel colours of mauve, yellow, green and pink with high windows and tiny balconies. Leafy trees provide shade to the rough cobblestones of the square, an oasis of classic neocolonial tranquility. It's not far from the train to Corcovado (*see* page 75) while down from the same station, in the Rua Cosme Velho, is the **Bica da Rainha** (Queen's mineral spring) where in the 19th century Dona Carlota Joaquina, the wife of the king, and her mother-in-law Queen Maria I, used to delicately splash their royal cheeks. The water from the spring was later put in barrels and sold in the city for its supposed life-restoring properties. The *largo* is named after the apothecary **Luís da Silva Souto** and its residents have gone to considerable trouble to maintain and restore its houses. To the extent of rescuing granite doors, tiles and other historically worthwhile items, from areas being demolished downtown to make way for tunnels, skyscrapers, freeways and reclaimed land.

Rua Cosme Velho descends to Rua das Laranjeiras. Off the latter is Rua General Glicério, an antique street where the 1880s textile factory **Companhia de Fiaçóes e Ticidas Aliança** used to be. You can visit two palaces in this area. In Rua Pinheiro Machado there is the **Palácio da Guanabara**. It looks like a many-tiered white and beige wedding cake. It was first occupied in 1865 by newlyweds Princess Isabel (daughter of the Emperor Pedro II) and Count D'Eu. It was in this palace that the Princess confirmed the Ministry of Justice's *Lei Áurea,* freeing Brazil's slaves. It has had several revamps and in 1910 became Brazil's presidential residence. It has lovely gardens and gilded interiors.

The other palace is the **Palácio Laranjeiras** in Rua Gago Coutinho with its magnificent iron gates, in the wooded park and gardens called Guinle, on the old Carvalho de Sá farm. This former presidential palace is seriously over the top: curved slate roofs, carrara marble staircase, granite from Bohemia, columns of onyx, huge French windows, Italian mosaic floor. It is jam-packed with priceless furniture, Persian rugs, tapestries and looks out over sculpted avenues of trees and fountains. Businessman Eduardo Guinle knew how to spend.

The two major **football** teams in Rio are **Flamengo** and **Fluminense**. The latter is over 100 years old and was the first soccer club in Rio. Its headquarters are in Laranjeiras, near Guanabara Palace. The club offers a total of some 20 sporting activities includng judo, basketball and water polo.

There are some real **shopping** treats in the Laranjeiras area. For Brazilian crafts try the **Pé de Boi**, one of the colourful houses in Rua Ipiringa.

GHOST STORY

An old house in Laranjeiras, the **Casa de Leitura**, was abandoned for so long that the neighbourhood began to suspect it was haunted. Nowadays, spruced-up, it is haunted only by those who come to read in its library. But late at night, when the lights at the reading tables are low, who knows?

COURTYARD MARKET

There are many Bohemian nooks in Rio. However, one with more claim than most is the **São José Market** in Laranjeiras. The market has various arts, crafts, crêpes, seafood and chopp around an open courtyard.

Below: *Guinle Park in Laranjeiras – forests, palms, gardens and the exotic Palácio Laranjeiras.*

11
Zona Norte

Central is a huge railway station just off Av Presidente Vargas. It is basically the dividing point between Centro, Zona Sul and the low-lying northern satellite towns. It includes many depressed and intensely populated areas as you will see coming in from the international airport. The church on your right on a bare hilltop, floodlit at night as if floating above the flatlands around it, is **Igreja Nossa Senhora da Penha**. Cut into the ascent rock are 365 steps which pilgrims climb up on their knees in October, the festival month. It is situated on the site of the old 1632 hermitage. Much of Rio's population lives in the north. It is a not very attractive urban sprawl, compensated for in many instances by its delightful people, ordinary working-class folk who are inevitably interested in and helpful towards visitors.

MERCADÃO DE MADUREIRA
To Market, To Market **

If you're in Copacabana take the metro, line one, from Siqueira Campos as far as Central Metro Station. Then change to the mainline train. Remember that the metro's orange seats are for pregnant women and the elderly. On the train itself, illegal food vendors hawk their tasty treats then nip off the train before a guard spots them. (The banana cream bite in chocolate is decadent.) You will rock slowly past house after house, electricity wires hanging like spaghetti everywhere. You pass 15 stations before you get to **Madureira** (double check when buying your ticket). You will emerge on a

Opposite: *An exotic carnaval-samba girl sings, dances and flirts with the crowds.*

Above: *Mercadão de Madureira – a feast of Amazon-size bargains.*

bridge. Here you should ask for Av Ministro Edgard Romero, the main crowded street. At No. 239 is the **Mercadão de Madureira** (Madureira Market) – a vast market several stories high, but with a rather inauspicious entrance. It sells everything, and at 30–40% less than elsewhere in Rio. Even the hawkers and street vendors come here to buy. The folk here are focused, busy and trying to survive. The shoes are at give-away prices, likewise the t-shirts emblazoned with a municipal school badge so that you can travel free on the trains. Here is where you will need your Portuguese phrase book, although sign language and a smile always seem to work.

Incense and Delectables **

Madureira has some 30 **Candomblé shops**, selling all those arcane potions and artifacts used in Afro-Brazilian religious ceremonies. Try **O Mundo Dos Orixás** (World of Gods). Here Hélio Sillman, who organizes the Yemanjá Goddess of the Sea Festival at Copacobana each year, will offer you candles decorated with effigies of Christian saints, fabulous headdresses of pearls and gold, incense for the lovelorn, cowries, walking sticks with devil heads, beads and fiery Bahia condiments. But the market is not all Candomblé. There are sugared-fruit shops, wine cellars, great cones of manioc, 18th-century slave dresses. Have an *a-kilo* lunch and a beer at one of the restaurants in the complex at half the price of downtown Rio; you may have to sit through a rerun of last night's soap though. All is fair exchange, no robbery in Madureira, a small-purse and big-heart market. Bring a backpack for your purchases.

SUCCULENT SUCOS

These drinks are made as you stand and wait.
- *manga* (mango)
- *cajú* (cashew); lovely to eat as well
- *pitanga*; good as an anti-diuretic.
- *guaraná*; from the Amazon
- *fruta do Conde* (custard apple)
- carambola (sweet and sour)
- *açerola*; full of vitamin C
- *maracujá* (passion fruit)

SÃO CRISTÓVÃO
Quinta da Boa Vista and Museu Nacional **

If you go back on the metro towards town, get off at São Cristóvão (it's also a metro stop). Right opposite is the **Quinta da Boa Vista**, former residence and private park of the emperor in the 19th century. His palace is now the **Museu Nacional** (National Museum). The museum is open 10:00–16:00, Tuesday–Sunday. It has a bit of everything, including exhibits devoted to the many peoples of Brazil: from Cariocas to cowboys, fishermen, Amazon Indians and priests of the Candomblé religion. The entrance hall features the 5360kg (11,819lb) **Bendegó meteorite** that fell to earth in Bahia in 1888.

The Quinta da Boa Vista, like so many parks around the world, is a colourful mix of football players and fast-food sellers, trees, lakes, children and Hyde-Park-like orators. City folk come here to relax, gossip and compare notes. There's a **zoo**, a **fauna museum** and a good **aviary** of colourful tropical birds. Small children are admitted free.

MUSIC AND DANCE

- **Samba:** the first samba song was the 1917 *Pelo Telefoné*. Carmen Miranda made samba world famous.
- **Bossa nova:** the new spirit. Born in the Zona Sul. Slower than samba. Vinícius de Moraes and Tom Jobim wrote *The Girl From Ipanema*.
- ***Pagode:*** popular TV and radio recordings are known as *pagode*. Samba rhythm.
- ***Forró:*** Rio's *favela* dwellers love their *forró*.
- **Breakdance** and **funk:** Brazilians in New York basically invented breakdance.
- Plus: *chorinho, sertanejo,* country and western, beach music, *tropicalismo,* axé, rock, *carimbo* of the Amazon, M&B (Brazilian Pop), electronic rock and even superb opera.

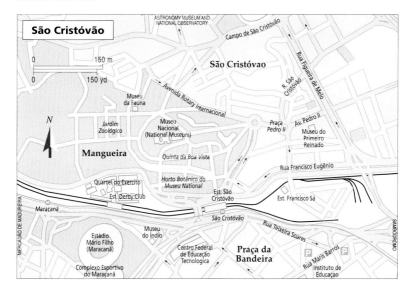

Below: *A ticket to football fever at Maracanã.*

Other places of interest in São Cristóvão include the
Astronomy Museum and **National Observatory**, founded
in 1827, in Rua General Bruce, and if you are still not
museum-sated, the **Military Museum** in Avenida Pedro II.
Sunday is a good day to go to the North Zone, as the
Feira de Nordeste (Northeast Fair) is held in **São
Cristóvão** at the Campo de São Cristóvão on that day.

Maracanã **
We have all watched **football** matches. Maradona,
Beckham, Thiery, Figo and Brazil's favourite sons
Ronaldo and Pelé. But you have not seen football until
you have watched a top-team Brazilian game. There
are drums, singing, flags, insults thrown at the ref (one
even had a wheelbarrow tipped on him at a match),
fights, fast food, team shirts, colour and dancing.

Maracanã Stadium or officially Estádio Mário Filho
can hold 185,000 making it possibly the world's largest
stadium. You can buy cheap tickets and stand, but it's a
bit rough. The expensive ones, the *arquibancadas*, are
on the terraces midfield. Halfway through the match,
one elderly gent regularly entertains the fans by coming
uninvited onto the field and for 15 minutes keeps a football in the air with his deft kicks, never once dropping it.
When a goal is scored a huge TV screen explodes with
the word 'GOOOOOL' as does the fast-talking whip-
up-the-excitement commentator. Designed for the 1950
World Cup, **Maraca**, as it is also known, has always
hosted the tense 'Fla-Flu' matches between Rio rivals
Flamengo and Fluminense. In 1925
the Brazilian international side consisted totally of players from these
two clubs. Inside the huge complex
there are olympic track and field
areas as well as a sports museum. It
also houses the sidewalk of fame
with the signatures and concrete
footprints of such Brazilian greats as
Pelé, Didi, Mané Garrincha, Zico
and Romário.

CARNAVAL ★★★

See Carnaval and die. It is the blood and guts and soul of Rio. Experience the ferocious drums, sensual samba and skimpy feathered costumes. Float after float. And a dancing, singing cast of tens of thousands. Revelry and laughter, band upon band, the lights, the streets, the whole of the

Above: *Carnaval is a ten-hour whirl of costume, colour, music and dance.*

city alive with people, music and ecstatic noise. Everyone loves everyone else during Carnaval, everybody is in a wild party mood. There is nothing like it anywhere else in the world. Combine Moulin Rouge in Paris, America's drum majorettes, Britain's Grenadier Guards, massed calisthenics in Beijing, Olympic opening ceremonies and World Cup Football and it still won't equate to Carnaval.

Carnaval is a veritable nuclear explosion of music, dance, colour, social message and fun in which 70,000 people exuberate.

The Mists of Time

Practically every society from the beginning of time has had **fertility festivals**, whether to celebrate planting the year's new crops or to pray for human fecundity. There have always been those who disapproved on grounds of public morality, but they have inevitably been overwhelmed by the sheer enthusiasm and joy of the people. Carnaval has always been a western Christian celebration. Street parades and theme floats, bands and masked balls were popular all over Europe in the late middle ages. Carnaval in old Italian means the last almighty rave-up prior to forsaking or removing meat, *carnelevare*, before the 40 fasting days of lent, leading up to Easter Sunday. There are echoes of it in the fasting and feasting of Islam's Ramadan. Officially Carnaval

BEST OF BAHIA

Each Carnaval School includes a huge troupe of swirling ladies dressed in the long, extravagant dresses of old plantation days. Known as the *Baianas*, they are there to salute old Salvador in Bahia where the parades first started. It was adopted by Carnaval in 1960. The women are all older and the pressure of the dance and non-stop singing can result in tragedy: in 1970 the much loved Mangueira Bahia lady, Nair Pequena, collapsed and died on Samba Avenue.

Sambódromo

Canal do Mangue

Avenida Presidente Vargas

Rua Benedito Hipólito

Praça Onze

Rua Prof. Clementino Fraga

Rua Julio Carmo

Sector 1

Rua Marquês de Pombal

Sector 5

Rua Carmo Neto

N

Rua Marquês do Sapucaí

Sector 2

Sector 7

Rua São Martinho

Tr. Pedregais

Rua Pres. Barroso

Museu da
Academia de Polícia

Sector 9

Rua T. Rabelo

Avenida Salvador de Sá

Sector 11

Rua dos Coqueiros

Sector 4

Tr. 11 de Maio

Rua H. Carrilho

Rua Senhor do Matozinhos

Praça Dona
Antónia

Ld. Frеi Orlando

0   150 m

Sector 13

0   150 yd

Sector 6

[i]

Museu do
Carnaval

lasts for five days, from Friday to Shrove Tuesday. Ash Wednesday, the beginning of lent, was when everyone was crossed with ashes on the forehead to remind man of the dust from whence he came and to which he would return. In fact Carnaval in Rio can start weeks earlier and for some it never really ends.

Carnaval came to Rio via Portuguese immigrants from the mid-Atlantic islands of Cabo Verde and Madeira. At the time it consisted of a mild dousing of one's neighbour with water or flour, and was accompanied by much laughter. The first parade in Rio was in 1786, percussion bands were later added and the first samba school was launched in the working-class suburb of Estácio in 1928. Carnaval parade was initially held in one of several streets in Rio with competition for selection intense. Finally it moved to the more formal Sambodrómo in 1984. Africa and its music and vivacity has had a huge influence on Carnaval, and it is probably true to say that the poorer and darker the neighbourhood, the better the samba school.

Bandas and Street Carnavals **

Not everyone approved of moving Rio's street carnavals to centralized Sambodrómo Stadium, so there are plenty of *bandas* (marching bands) rehearsing in the streets long before the official processions. And increasingly these more amateur offshoots are coming into their own. You can join in the procession, hundreds do. There are open *banda* parades all over Rio – in Copacabana, Leme, Av Rio Branco, Boulevard 28, Setembro – often on Saturdays before and during Carnaval or on Carnaval Saturday itself. The most hilarious are the two in Ipanema, **Banda Carmen Miranda** and **Banda de Ipanema** – gays, drag queens, transvestites, some of the funniest and best individual acting you will ever see. These *bandas* started in the 1960s as a two-finger gesture to the then military regime.

Samba Schools ***

There are 14 Special Group Samba Schools (let alone the rest) with an average of 5000 performers, dancers and instrumentalists in each group. There is a very distinct hierarchy in each school. They train like Olympic athletes for six months prior to Carnaval.

Pecking order in each school starts with the schools's president. In the past they were often crime bosses polishing their public relations. Then comes the *velha guarda* (old guard members), followed by the

CARNAVAL AND CITIZENSHIP

There is a permanent exhibition of costumes and display photos covering the many years of Carnaval in the new **Carnaval and Citizenship Cultural Center**, in the Sambodrómo. It is here that workshops of the various samba schools give training lessons to folk from low-income communities, teaching them float construction and design. In the shop you can also buy drums and tambourines made by the students.

GREAT TRAIN ROBBER

Britain's great train robber, Ronald Biggs, perfected one of the most daring robberies in England since Dick Turpin. Caught, jailed, he escaped to Rio de Janeiro under the pseudonym Michael Haynes where he was to live for the next 30 years with his Carioca wife and family. Eventually in 2001 for health reasons he gave himself up to the British Police and returned home.

Opposite: *The prettiest and most vivacious girl on the block carries her group's flag.*
Left: *Hundreds of lovingly made costumes, with matching drums and tambourines. Everyone singing.*

Joãosinho Trinta's creativity
enabled him to win seven
out of ten of his first
Carnaval parades. Claiming
to have been born as a result
of a good Carnaval fling by
his mother, the maestro
basically revolutionized
Carnaval. He is also quoted
as saying that only Brazilians
could have created an event
like the Carnaval parade:
'...because we're crazy. I've
travelled the world over,' he
says, 'I've seen magnificent
and breathtaking things, but
only Rio has all the beauty
and emotion worthy of the
title The Wonderful City.'

carnavalesco (carnaval master) who is the creative
genius behind the theme and design of the floats.
Chubby, silver- haired Joãosinho Trinta is considered
the best. He began his reign in 1974 with his 'King of
France on the Haunted Island' for the Salgueiro School,
which won the championship. He has won many acco-
lades since and in 2004 was even featured on the cover
of Rio's *Samba e Carnaval* magazine.

The inevitably gorgeous girl in sequined bikini and
peacock feathers who flies the flag and leads each
school's contingent is known as the *porta bandeira*.
Among those who have made Miss World look tame have
been the smiling Selminha Sorriso. The drummers' muses
who inspire their schools with their beauty and laughter as
they samba among the floats, have been such lovelies as
Luma de Oliveira, Luana Piovani, Deborah Secco and TV
star and darling of Rio, Juliana Paes. The performance of
the flag bearer and her male escort, the first couple, often
determines which school obtains the coveted 10 points.

Rehearsals **

You can get a good taste of Carnaval by going along to
any *ensaios* (rehearsals) August–February; but from
Christmas onwards it's difficult to get in. Praça Mauá
on Saturday nights is worthwhile, as many schools have
their workshops here.

Carnaval Balls *

Fancy-dress balls at Carnaval
range from the elegant and
grand affairs at Copacabana
Palace and Ipanema's Caesar
Park, to the spectacularly
licentious. They start at about
23:00 and end with breakfast.
What goes on in between is
enough to boggle the mind
with its musical adaptability,
romantic encounters and feasting propensity of Dionysius.

Left: *Carnaval Parade: one of the greatest extravaganzas on earth.*
Opposite: *Sequins, spice and all that is nice; pearls and twirls and beautiful girls.*

Carnaval Parade ★★★

You can buy tickets at Travel Agencies, Maracanã Stadium or check with your hotel. Tickets for Carnaval weekend are usually sold out way in advance but you can pick up scalpers' tickets if you arrive late.

The parade is held along the **Rua Marquês de Sacupai** in the Sambodrómo watched by lucky ticket holders on tiered platforms and lasts about 10 hours with each of the 14 top groups parading for just over an hour. The whole extravaganza starts with an explosion of fireworks and the haunting samba war cry of the *puxador.*

There can be 6000 performers in each group. Each group is in turn subdivided into *alas* (wings) featuring floats and different (and unbelievably colourful) costumes. Each school has its specially composed samba and school theme. The beat is catchy and the drumming non-stop. The drum group in each school, the *bateria*, can number as many as 350 instruments.

Older women dressed in the historical slaves' dresses of Bahia swirl and twirl, younger laughing women dance practically naked, individuals entertain the crowds, the floats come alive, the cachaça rum flows and everyone is singing and dancing in a fabulous display of costume and colour. That's Carnaval of Zona Norte.

COP A PLEA

If revellers get too rowdy at Carnaval, the long hand of the law is nearby. A special Criminal Station has been set up right on Samba (Sacupai) Avenue with a judge on duty, prosecutor and civil police officers. The good news for merrymakers is that a public defender is also at hand nearby to plead that it was all only good clean fun.

KING MOMO

King Momo kicks off the Carnaval Parade. With the Queen and Princess. Momo comes from ancient Greco-Roman mythology. Being the god of irreverence, he was banished from Mount Olympus, only to re-emerge in Rio in 1933.

12
Beyond Rio

Nestling in the **Serra do Mar**, the mountains 60km (40 miles) inland from Rio de Janeiro, are three resort towns: **Nova Friburgo**, **Petrópolis** and **Teresópolis**.

PETRÓPOLIS

To get to Petrópolis catch a luxury bus from Rodoviária Station for under R$15. The journey up the winding, forested and occasionally misty mountain road takes an hour. Petrópolis, Imperial City and City of Hydrangeas became the summer capital for the court when **Emperor Dom Pedro** first visited the town, loved it and, encouraged by his wife Dona Amélia, bought a large property, **Córrego Seco**, there in 1830. Petrópolis, the route from the interior for gold and coffee exports to Rio Port, was named after him. Its cool climate and lack of yellow fever made it a haven for those who could afford it. Its highest temperature average is 23ºC (73ºF) and at night in winter it can drop to freezing.

Surprisingly (as it looks like a village), Petrópolis has a population of 300,000. It lies in a valley of three rivers which in the historic centre have been channelled to run down and divide the main *avenidas*. Graced with flowering trees, orchids and scenery, Petrópolis is a champagne-air garden town.

Bohemia

Emperor Pedro I abdicated in 1831 in favour of his son in order to return to a fractious Portugal. Thus he never actually got to build his summer palace. The

DON'T MISS

*** Ferry to Niterói: an hour's walk to the Museum of Modern Art.
*** Historical Petrópolis: a stroll in a gracious town.
** Imperial Museum, Petrópolis: take a horse-drawn cab to the old Summer Palace of the Emperor.
* Crystal Palace, Petrópolis: in lovely gardens.
* Orquidario Binot orchid gardens: take a taxi.
* Street food: try any food but meat. Always drink bottled water.

Opposite: *Niterói's museum of Modern Art competes with Sugar Loaf across Guanabara Bay.*

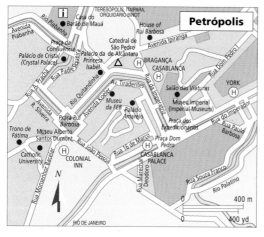

Petrópolis

development of his property was left to **Major Júlio Frederico Koeler**, a German immigrant who had been constructing roads to the neighbouring Minas Gerais mines (at one time the source of 50% of the world's gold). It was Koeler who suggested that German immigrants be encouraged to settle and develop **Córrego Seco**, now the town's historic centre. To this day quite a few of the Petrópolis residents look German, speak German and have German sounding restaurants and shops. It was not until 1843, however, that the new emperor, **Dom Pedro II**, agreed to the idea, with the proviso that a summer palace and town also be constructed. This was pursued with German efficiency under the supervision of the imperial butler **Paulo Barbosa**. A well laid out town with gracious residences developed, particularly when the emperor and his court decided that Petrópolis was the best place to escape Rio's humidity.

Brazil's German community was also much involved in the construction of the country's first railway. Built in 1854, it linked Porto Mauá in Rio's Guanabara Bay with Raiz da Serra, affording easy access to Petrópolis. Thirty years later it reached Petrópolis itself. In 1889 the Brazilian Republic was declared. By this time Petrópolis had become an important administrative centre. It was the Rio state capital from 1894–1903 and in the following year became the official summer residence of the president, the palace of the former Baron of Rio Negro, becoming his Petrópolis pied-à-terre. In 1928 Petrópolis and Rio were connected by the country's first tarmac road. Tourism was big in the 1940s when Petrópolis' Casino attracted the famous and frivolous from all over

FORESTS OF RAIN

Ecologists believe there is little point in lecturing Brazil on deforestation in the Amazon, particularly if one considers the appalling destruction of Europe's great forests in centuries past. Far better to promote such projects as the Amazon Reserves and Protected Areas partnership between Brazil and the World Bank, and put your money where your green heart is.

CASA DO COLONO

Museu Casa do Colono, on Rua Cristóvão Colombo, is an 1847 colonist's house built by German settler **Johan Gottlieb Kaiser**. The walls of the cottage are of wattle and daub and the interior is still how it was left 150 years ago. (Closed Mondays.)

the world. Tourism is still central today but considerable industry, particularly beer-making, has developed.

Petrópolis offers umpteen visitor tours including horse riding, climbing, mushroom farms, coffee *fazenda* visits, ecotourisim, trout fishing, boating, organic herbal gardens, a full calendar of musical events and even balls in the Crystal Palace for third-agers (over 60's). It has excellent restaurants and elegant boutiques.

Centro Histórico ★★★

The centre of the historic town or Centro Histórico is **Praça Rui Barbosa**, just below the hilltop Catholic University. There is an information centre, a big circular fountain and leading off it a series of channels linking and channelling the three rivers that make this town such a delight: Palatino, Quitandinha and Piabanha. The square faces the lofty 80-year-old Gothic spire of the **Catedral de São Pedro de Alcântara** with its tombs of Dom Pedro II and his empress, Teresa Cristina, and that of Princess Regent Dona Isabel. As with many Brazilian attractions it is closed on Monday. Just behind it in Av Ipiranga, is the former house (now a private residence) of Brazilian composer **Rui Barbosa**.

The Imperial Museum ★★

Walk southeast along Av Tiradentes then cross the little bridge onto Rua da Imperatriz until you come to the **Imperial Museum** in the old neo-classical **Summer Palace** with its lovely parklands. You'll be given a pair of felt over-slippers (slippery marble) to walk through rooms of rich furniture, porcelains, the Royal Crown (639 diamonds in gold) and even the imperial loo. They are all still there as if in a time warp throwback to 15 November 1889, when a bloodless republican coup overthrew the monarchy and the

GUNPOWDER PLOT

When the Portuguese royals arrived in Rio in 1808, they wondered if they would need to defend their South American empire from Napoleon. So the first thing they did was take over the sugar-cane mill near Lagoa Rodrigo de Freitas and build a gunpowder factory in what is today the Botanical Gardens. But after one too many explosive mishaps they banished it inland to Petrópolis in the mountains in 1831.

Below: *The gracious multi-salon Museu Imperial.*

MUD AND GLORY

5000 Brazilian troops fought in Italy in World War II, the only South American country to do so. A memorial to the expeditionary force can be found in Avenida Koeler in Petrópolis, in the form of a small museum called the **Museu da FEB**, or **Forca Expedicionária Brasileira**. Closed on Tuesdays.

MOUNTAIN ORCHIDS

If you are interested in orchids, Petrópolis is famous for them. Take a taxi and visit the 140-year-old private orchid gardens of **Orquidário Binot** in Retiro suburb, 390 Rua Fernandes Vieira. It is closed from 11:00–13:00 and on Sundays. The Binot family still run it and it was Binot himself who designed the garden of the Imperial Palace.

emperor had to make a hurried exit. In the separate Salão das Viaturas, the old Leopoldina railway loco sits proud and polished. It linked Rio and Petrópolis for 81 years until 1964. There is a teashop.

The Crystal Palace **

Within walking distance of the museum is the **Crystal Palace** (Palácio de Cristal) off the Rua Alfredo Pachá, a smaller version of Joseph Paxton's Crystal Palace built for Queen Victoria's Great Exhibition of 1851. All glass and iron, they became the rage in 19th-century Europe. The Petrópolis version, which is lit up at night, was built in France in 1879 and soon became the imperial ballroom. Among its fountains, flowers and lawns, you'll hear the shrill cries of green parakeets feeding on the fruit of lofty palms. Brumelias with their red and green leaves and red flowers are everywhere.

Walkabout ***

There are six tourism information centres in Petrópolis. One is in the elegant residence of **Barão de Mauá** very near the Crystal Palace. Just opposite in Rua Alfredo Pachá is the **Bohemian Brewery** that has been making what is probably Brazil's best German-like Pilsener since 1853. A beer festival is held here in June.

Back at **Liberdade Square**, walk for two minutes up

Rua Barão do Amazonas, turn right and there above you on the hillside is the white, blue-shuttered and red-roofed chalet of aviation pioneer **Alberto Santos Dumont**. The fairytale house, now a museum, is known as *A Encantada* (The Enchanted One). Rio's regional airport is named after aviator and hot-air balloon pioneer Dumont, who first flew his own aircraft for all of seven seconds on

23 October 1906. Right in front of you as you look up at Dumonts' house is a large clock of shrubs and flowers cut into the uphill lawns that lead to the **Catholic University of Petrópolis**, and higher still to the **Quinta do Sol** viewsite. If you're tired of walking, take a horse and open carriage to clip-clop around the rest of the sights.

TERESÓPOLIS AND NOVA FRIBURGO

Another mountain resort is **Teresópolis** in the **Serra dos Órgãos National Park** (the rock formations are said to resemble organ pipes). At 910m (3003ft) it is the highest town in the State of Rio. Its **Pedra do Sino** (Bell Rock) reaches up to 2263m (7470ft). There's a path to the top. **Nova Friburgo** is where riding enthusiasts go. The resort was founded in 1818 by 300 Swiss families from Fribourg.

Above: *The leisurely Niterói ferry with the Brazilian flag waving in the breeze.*
Opposite: *The gardens of the Crystal Palace, Petropólis.*

NITERÓI

The ferry ride from downtown Rio to Niterói across Guanabara Bay is a great day's excursion. As the old ferry chugs along past the Bavarian **Ilha Fiscal Castle** there are gorgeous views of Rio behind you. Planes take off non-stop from Santos Dumont Airport.

Niterói looks like an island or even a part of Rio itself but in fact it is a separate city. It means 'concealed waters' in the Indian Tupi-Guarani language. French settlers were the first to occupy the area but were quickly ejected by the Portuguese who in 1573 formally named it **São Lourenço**, and allowed their ally, the son of the Tamininó chief Arabiboía, to settle here. It was only in 1834 that it was renamed Niterói and in 1902 it became the capital of Rio de Janeiro State.

Ricota Fresca and Flying Saucers **

When you disembark, turn right along the seafront until you are clear of the rather unprepossessing buildings near the ferry terminal. You will soon come to a smaller

---

TROPICAL DELIGHT

If you love her, present her with a spray of orchids. One in every 14 flowering plants in the world is an orchid. Some grow in the ground, others, known as epiphytes, grow on trees. Colour and scent are the two ways an orchid attracts pollinating insects. Some orchids bloom to blush for one day only, others for months. Orchids have been cultivated since the times of the Chinese philosopher Confucious 2500 years ago and in Europe from the end of the 18th century. *Salep*, an extract from the roots of some orchids, is used in the Middle East as a hot drink.

Above: *The Museum of Modern Art perches like a sci-fi flying saucer on a Niterói bluff.*

coastal road with a haggle of small brightly painted houses laced with the ubiquitous overhead electricity cables. Further on, fishermen with their rods sit in chairs on the sidewalk beneath flowering trees. In the distance across the water Rio shimmers in the heat. You then go uphill, stopping perhaps to buy a little *ricota fresca* (a white soft cheese eaten with compressed guava jelly) from the back of a panel van. Or if you're hungry enough, one of the skateboard-sized Minas Gerais cheeses. Be sure to take a water bottle for the walk from the ferry.

On the crest of the hill an extraordinary white flying saucer comes into view. This is the **Museu Arte Contemporânea** (Museum of Modern Art) or more commonly MAC, designed by Oscar Niemeyer and opened in 1996. It is an incredible piece of architecture perched on the cliff edge, overlooking the small beach of Boa Viagem, and in the near distance the suburb and sweep of Icaraí Promenade. The MAC is an architecturally startling building full of light, symmetry and Niemeyer's creative genius. As you walk around, the inside balcony offers 360º views of Guanabara Bay, Niterói and Rio. The sea below is a favourite with hand-line fishermen in small boats.

Niterói Area

0 ————— 5 km
0 ——— 2.5 miles   Baía de Guanabara   Ilha Santa Cruz   São Gonçalo

Ilha do Fundão   Neves   Sete Pontes
                        BR 101
São Cristóvão   RIO DE JANEIRO   Niterói
Quinta da   Ilha das Cobras
Boa Vista   Ilha Fiscal   Muesu Arte
                Castle   Contemporánea
Centro   (Musem of Modern Art)   Icaraí
                        Praia de Icaraí
            AEROPORTO   Praia de São
Tijuca   SANTOS DUMONT   Franciseo   Praia de
                    Praia do   Charitas
Glória   Flamengo   Charitas
                Urca   Fortaleza de   Lagoa de
Corcovado Redentor   Santa Cruz   Piratininga
  (Christ the   Praia de   O
704 m Redeemer)   Pão de Açúcar   Imubi
                (Sugar Loaf)   Praia de
Lagoa   Ilha de Cotunduba   Piratininga
Rodrigo   Copacabana
de Freitas

More Beaches ★

Icaraí is the first large beach you come to, with the usual ladies' volleyball classes underway on the sand. Icaraí and its neigh-bouring beaches **São Francisco** and **Charitas** are popular restaurant and nightlife areas, but the beaches further around the coast are better.

Take a taxi to the **Fortaleza de Santa Cruz** beyond Icaraí. This fort, built 400 years ago to guard the mouth of the bay, contains gun batteries, massive concrete pillboxes and even a macabre execution site.

There are other smaller **museums** in Niterói, two ancient **forts** and several colonial **churches** dating back as far as 1627. **Yachting** is popular in this less crowded, relaxed neighbour of Rio and there are at least three yacht clubs. Some commuters who work in Rio prefer Niterói's quiet more relaxed lifestyle in which to live, even though it means crossing the bay each day by ferry, hydrofoil or even driving over the 14km (9-mile) Niterói Bridge that links these two arms of Guanabara Bay.

OFF TO THE COUNTRY

Take a day and a night and travel by car or bus to a variety of lovely seaside resorts east and west of Rio.

The Costa do Sol **

The **Costa do Sol** to the northeast includes the fishing villages of Maricá, Saquarema, Araruama Lake, Arraial do Cabo, and some 160km (100 miles) from Rio, Cabo Frio with its dunes and unspoilt beaches. Most popular with Cariocas and crowded with 130,000 visitors in summer, is **Buzios** with its 25 beaches.

Below: *The bridge linking Rio and Niterói stretches 14km (9 miles) across Guanabara Bay.*

The Costa Verde **

The **Costa Verde** south-west of Rio is accessed some 150km (95 miles) along the Atlantic-flanked and forested Rio-Santos highway. **Angra dos Reis** was first founded in 1502

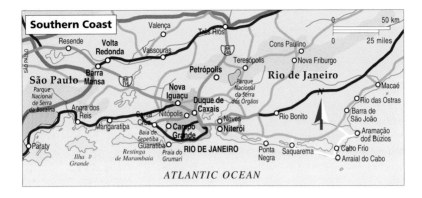

on a huge bay dimpled with islands. Opposite is **Ilha Grande**, reached by ferry. It is Emerald Coast at its most pristine, lush Atlantic rainforest sweeping down its many mountains. Once a haunt of pirates, then a prison island, it is now a state park.

Casa do Pontal *

In the southeast corner of **Praia da Barra da Tijuca** is the **Praia dos Bandeirantes**. The *bandeirantes* were slave raiders whose pioneering travels deep into the Brazilian jungles resulted in the opening up of the country. This is the area where they used to R & R or *recreio*. A promontory, **Morro do Pontal**, which you can reach at low tide, leads out to sea.

Take the Estrada do Pontal and weave your way along a forest-canopied road to the tree-hidden villa called **Casa do Pontal**, a folk-art museum. Its fascinating miniatures, largely of baked clay, come from all over Brazil and reflect every aspect of rural and city life including festivals, dancing, romance, marriage, industrial strikes, religious festivals, and technological triumphs. It is in effect a child's wonderland of what makes Brazil. Though it is the largest and most important museum of folk sculpture art in Rio, you are quite likely to be one of the few people there. There are over 8000 pieces usually set in groups, each of which tell an amusing or sad and sometimes frightening story. All the

FLAGS AND JESUITS

The *bandeirantes*, so called because they grouped themselves under different flags, were responsible for opening up the vast *sertão* or interior of Brazil. The motivation of these pioneer adventurers was not altogether benign. They deliberately went out to capture Indian slaves. Jesuit *aldeias* or missions saved some Indians, but many died from the new European diseases. The Jesuits became too independently powerful, were outmanoeuvred by the sugar and coffee barons and mining magnates, and were banished in 1759.

pieces of art were collected by French-born **Jacques van de Beuque** from 200 Brazilian artists over 50 years (1950–2000). It is an anthropological feast reflecting the totality of life and culture of the many peoples of Brazil. There's even an action miniature samba band and floats. The museum has exhibited in 14 countries.

Hideaways *

Make your way back to the mountainous coastal road and you'll pass the little **Prainha Cove** where the young people of Rio surf. It looks out over islands, palms and rock fishermen in an environmental protection area where residential construction is forbidden. A welcome relief after Barra. There is a park with trails and scenic viewpoints. The 4km (2-mile) amphitheatre of **Grumari Beach** is also a protected rainforest area and free of development. Along the Estrada da Barra de Guaratiba is the **Burle Marx Villa**, home of the famous landscape artist from 1949–94, with its garden of over 3000 plant species. The lovely verandah'd residence also houses his pre-Columbian and religious art, as well as sculpture and paintings by Burle Marx himself.

Back at Av Estado da Guanabara, on top of the hill overlooking the vast mangrove swamp of **Marambaia** and protected by a sand-dune ridge and sweep of blue ocean that seems to stretch forever, is the **Arumari Restaurant**. The restaurant also hovers over the sleepy little fishing village of **Guaratiba** where retired police officers choose to live and where there are no hotels among its cluster of modest hill holiday residences. The perfect hideaway. Pause at one of the tiny roadside restaurants for a meal of whole grilled fish, *pirão*, chilli and rice washed down by a three-tot *caipirinha*.

THE DEEP BLUE SEA
• **Board surfing**: Prainha de Grumari, Barra da Tijuca, São Conrado, Arpoador
• **Scuba diving**: Ilhas Cagarras, Ilha Grande (Ubatuba Vermelha, dos eros)
• **Rock fishing**: Leme, Copacabana fort, Vermelha beach (Urca), Caboinhas (Niterói)
• **Sailing**: Barra da Tijuca, Botafogo
NB Keep your eye out for weather and current changes.

Below: *Grumari Beach. Stranger in paradise, all lost in a tropic land.*

Rio de Janeiro at a Glance

BEST TIMES TO VISIT

May, June, July and August to take advantage of the cooler winter months. You will need a coat or jersey at night. This is also the time of lowest rainfall and consequently lowest humidity. The summer months, particularly during Carnaval, are hot and humid with temperatures in January and February reaching 33ºC (92ºF). It is also rainy. Which just means you have to dash indoors at your pavement café to continue eating. There are no hurricanes, earthquakes, floods or volcanoes. The sea is always comfortable for swimming and the winds, although good for sailing, are never too strong. Rio lies right on the Tropic of Capricorn.

GETTING THERE

By air: Rio is linked either directly or via São Paulo to nearly all the main European cities by their respective national carriers or by **Varig**, the Brazilian airline. At least seven US airlines fly into Rio from ten airports, as do flights from all South American countries. There are four flights a week from Johannesburg (change at São Paulo). Peak holiday times are mid-December to mid-January, Carnaval and mid-June to mid-August. Flights from Australia tend to go the south polar route. (Via Johannesburg is another option.) From Dubai the best connec-

tions are via Johannesburg. You land at **Antônio Carlos Jobim International Airport** (Galeão) which is 20 minutes from Rio by taxi. The airline luggage code for Rio is GIG and for São Paulo GRU.
On arrival change money at the **Banco do Brasil**, Floor 3, Terminal 1, with its Visa ATMs. There are Riotour desks for advice. Transcopass or Cootrama will call you a taxi (about US$25). Buy a ticket from them at their counter inside the arrivals hall, after collecting luggage. There are buses for less than US$4 but keep bus travel for later when you are more knowledgeable.
By road: There are **buses**, usually air conditioned and well maintained, from practically all of Rio's neighbouring countries and from many points within Brazil. The central bus station, **Rodoviária**, is just north of the city centre; tel: (21) 2291-5151.
If you are **driving**, you will need an international driving licence and passport. No special document is normally needed to bring in a car for up to 90 days other than proof of ownership and/or registration. Driving is on the right-hand side as in all of South America.
By sea: Other than luxury cruise vessels who only stay a short time, a variety of cargo boats leaving Europe do, at times, take passengers. If

arriving in your own vessel, immediately after you tie up, you should visit the Port Captain in **Espaço Cultural da Marinha**, Av Alfredo Agache, Centro. Then go to Customs.

GETTING YOUR BEARINGS

Rio is divided into three main zones: North, **Zona Norte** (pronounced *nortche*), and South, **Zona Sul** with downtown **Centro** separating them. Look up at the *Redentor* and you'll orientate yourself. His left arm points northwest and his right arm southeast. The dividing line between north and south is roughly the main railway station. Access to the international airport, up-country towns and São Paulo pass through Zona Norte. Centro is the city's business hub and historical heartland. The docks and the ferry departure point to Niterói are here. You will spend some of your time in Centro with its access routes to Sugar Loaf, Corcovado and Santa Teresa, but most in the south which encompasses the famous beaches of Copacabana and Ipanema. Further southeast are the Botanical Gardens and the huge Tijuca National Park.

GETTING AROUND

Walking is by far the best way to get to know Rio. You will quickly pick up the busy ambience of this food-, sport- and music-mad city.

Rio de Janeiro at a Glance

By air: domestic air routes within Brazil include some 40 destinations of which **Foz do Iguaçu**, the famous waterfalls and **Salvador** with its old houses, cobbled streets, Afro-Brazilian foods, crafts and religious ceremonies, should be top of your list. You can buy a discounted airpass (outside Brazil) covering several cities, from all international carriers.

By taxi: most taxis are yellow, reasonably priced, available at any corner and and nearly all have meters. They do not harass you as in some cities other than occasionally flash their lights. The drivers seldom speak English. You can order a taxi, 24 hours, by phoning, for example, **Transcoopas** (21) 2560-4888 or **Cootrama Radio Taxi** (21) 3976-9944. Negotiate with the driver and you may get a 30% discount from the city to the international airport.

By bus: excellent and regular services to all parts of Rio. At times half a dozen will arrive at once. Ask which bus stop to wait at and keep an eye on the destination written on top of the bus and on the side. Enter at the front, pay at a small turnstile and exit from the back after pressing the bell. The buses cost the same no matter the distance, and a little more if it is *ar condicionado*. Ask where to get off. Again don't expect much English. Most buses from Rodoviária heading south will take you to Copacabana.

By metro: open 06:00–23:00 daily. This fast modern air-conditioned subway has two lines. **Line One** (red) from Saens Peña in the west, loops through the city centre; 16 stops to Siquiera Campos within walking distance of Copa Beach. Buy your ticket at the ticket counter and if you ask for a combined metro-bus ticket *combinacião* you can then get a metro bus at Siquiera Campos to either Ipanema or Gávea (check the bus signs). Normally the ticket machine that opens the turnstile will gobble your ticket, not so if you have a *combinacião*. If you are heading for the southern end of Copacabana, press the bell once you pass Peter Pan Children's Park. **Line Two** (green) links up with Line One at Estácio where, if you are heading north to watch football at Maracanã, you change. The system is simple, the trains are spotless, the only drawbacks are that the stations seldom have the lovely wall art of Paris or London and there are no station loos. The trains are several blocks back from the beaches. You can buy multiple-ride tickets.

By train: one goes up to Corcovado from Rua Cosme Velho. The other is the tiny *bondinho* train up to Santa Teresa, near the big cathedral. There are plenty of commuter trains to Zona Norte.

By car: Rio's roads are excellent, cars seldom jump lights, and the standard of driving is high. But everyone yearns to be a Formula-One driver. Lanes mean nothing as the traffic weaves and flows at speed. It takes some getting used to if you are from a more law-and-order motoring culture. Service stations are usually closed on Sundays and often on Saturdays. Some cars, especially taxis, are fueled on alcohol and/or gas. With a credit card (essential) you can hire a car but they are quite expensive. Buy and resell rather than rent for a long period. Rental companies include, **Localiza**, tel: (21) 2275-3340, and **Avis**, tel: (21) 3398-5060 (Galeão Airport). You will need to be at least 25 years old. Check insurance.

By scooter, motorbike or bicycle: You can hire any of these in Rio. Bicycling is popular. Bicycle tracks or *ciclóvia* run past the popular beaches, the Rodrigo de Freitas Lake and at Barra da Tijuca. There is even one all the way from Leme to the centre of town.

By mini van: vans go from the town centre to Zona Sul as far as Barra da Tijuca. Frequent and quick. Look for the sign in front of the van.

By sea: ferries and the faster **catamaran** go from the ferry terminal at Barcas Station at Praça 15 to Niterói across the harbour every 10 minutes.

Rio de Janeiro at a Glance

There are several **yacht** clubs, mainly at the Urca and Glória waterfronts. Schooner cruises (*see* Tours and Excursions).

WHERE TO STAY

Arpoador
MID-RANGE
Arpoador Inn, 177 rua Francisco Otaviano, 177, tel: (21) 2523-0060, e-mail: arpoador@unisys.com.br Small inn between Copa and Ipanema right on beach. Fish restaurant.

Barra
LUXURY
Sheraton, Av Sernambetiba, 3.150, Barra da Tijuca, tel: (21) 3139-8000, e-mail: reserva.barra@sheraton.com Has a private beach out of town, plus all the usual Sheraton facilities.

Botafogo
LUXURY
Caesar Business Rio de Janeiro, 39 rua da Passagem, tel: (21) 2131-1212, www.caesarbusiness.com.br

Búzios
MID-RANGE
Pousada Tambaú de Búzios, Rua E2-Lote 64 – Condominio do Atlântico, Praia da Ferradura, Armaçao dos Búzios, tel: (22) 2623-4736, e-mail: tambaubuzios@ tambaubuzios.com.br www.tambaubuzios.com.br Overlooking the bay. Stepped duplex chalets.

Catete
MID-RANGE
Imperial, 186 rua do Catete, tel: (21) 2556-5212, e-mail: imperialhotel@skydone.net Old-colonial-residence feel.
Flórida, 81 rua Ferreira Viana, tel: (21) 2555-6000. The restaurant buffet is a favourite with local folk.

Centro
MID-RANGE
Guanabara Palace, 392 av Presidente Vargas, tel: (21) 2216-1313, e-mail: guanabara@windsorhoteis.com.br Free transfers to airport and Copacabana. Business hotel. Sauna.

Copacabana
LUXURY
Copacabana Palace, 1702 av Atlântica, tel: (21) 2548-7070, e-mail: reservations@ copacobanapalace.com.br www.copacabana palace.orient-express.com 1930s elegant grand deluxe.
Hotel Rio International, 1500 av Atlântica, tel: (21) 2546-8000, e-mail: reservas@ riointernational.com.br www.riointernational.com.br Mid-esplanade, palms by top-floor pool.
JW Marriott, 2600 av Atlântica, tel: (21) 2545-6500, e-mail: reserves.brasil@ marriotthotels.com www. marriotthotels.com/riomc Room safes suitable for laptops; 245 rooms including 140 non-smoking. Beach service.

Le Meridien, 1020 av Atlântica, tel: (21) 3873-8850, e-mail: reserves@ lemeridien-riodejaneiro.com www.lemeridien-copacabana.com. 496 rooms; business centre. Beach.
Sofitel Rio Palace, 4240 av Atlântica, tel: (21) 2525-1232, e-mail: sofitelrio@ accorhotels.com.br www.accor-hotels.com Wood-panelled bar, restaurant overlooking sea.

MID-RANGE
Orla Copacabana Hotel, 4122 av Atlântica, tel: (21) 2525-2425, e-mail: orla@ orlahotel.co.br www.orlahotel.com.br On Copacabana Beach near fort, Arpoador and Ipanema. Good prices, inclusive of huge breakfast. Recommended.
Augusto's Copacabana, 119 rua Bolivar, tel: (21) 2547-1800, e-mail: reservas@ augustos-hotel.com.br www.augustos-hotel.com.br Four blocks from the beach. Popular with Brazilian business men. Homelike.
Rio Copa, 370 av Princesa Isabel, tel: (21) 2275-6644, e-mail: riocopa@riocopa-com.br Surrounded by nightclubs. Switched-on informative staff. Near Rio Sul Shopping Mall.

BUDGET
Santa Clara Hotel, 316 rua Décio Vilares, tel: (21) 2256-2650, e-mail: reserva@

hotelsantaclara.com.br
www.hotelsantaclara.com.br
Simple rustic accommodation
back from the beach near
Siqueira Campos metro
station. Very quiet.

Flamengo
LUXURY
Novo Mundo, 20 Praia
do Flamengo, tel: (21)
2557-6226, www.
hotelnovomundo-rio.com.br
Situated near the former
Presidential Palace, with a
beautiful view of Flamengo
Park and Bay.

MID-RANGE
Éscorial, 135 rua Dois de
Dezembro, tel: (21) 2556-
9119. Well known to
businessmen. Nice small
rooms. Friendly staff.
Paysandu, 23 rua Paissandu,
tel: (21) 2558-7270,
e-mail: reservas@
paysanduhotel.com.br
Small cosy atmosphere.
Near Flamengo Promenade.

Glória
LUXURY
Hotel Glória, 632 rua do
Russel, tel: (21) 2555-7272,
e-mail:
hotel@hotelgloria.com.br
Grand, elegant hotel like
Copacabana Palace.

Ipanema
LUXURY
Caesar Park Rio de Janeiro,
460 av Viera Souto, tel:
(21) 2525-2525, www.

caesarpark.com.br Business
centre. Tower block on the
beach. Excellent.
Hotel Sol Ipanema, 320 av
Viera Souto, tel: (21) 2525-
2020, email: hotel@
solipanema.com.br
Evidence Restaurant, top-floor
pool. Best Western group.

MID-RANGE
Vermont, 254 rua Visconde
de Pirajá, tel: (21) 2522-0057,
e-mail: hoteisvermont@uol.
com.br Commercial heart
of 'Ipa'. Helpful staff. Surrounded by restaurants,
bars and buzz.

Laranjeiras
MID-RANGE
Serrano, 22 rua Gago
Coutinho, tel: (21) 2205-1846.
Small hotel tucked away from
the hubbub; close to restaur-
ants, shopping and transport.

Leblon
LUXURY
Marina Palace, 630 av Del-
phim Moreira, tel: (21) 2294-
1794, e-mail: hotelmarina@
hotelmarina.com.br Splendid
ocean view. Good nightlife
for the younger set.

MID-RANGE
Leblon Palace, 204 av Ataulfo
de Paiva, tel: (21) 2512-8000,
e-mail: leblonpalace@
leblonpalace.com.br
www.leblonpalace.com.br
On a main commercial street
on a busy boutique corner in
the fashionable area.

Petrópolis
MID-RANGE
There are 45 hotels and inns
in Petrópolis.
Colonial Inn, 125 rua Mon-
senhor Bacelar, telefax: PABX
(0242) 43-1590 · 31-2870.
Near historic centre, reasonably priced. Recommended.

Recreio dos Bandeirantes
LUXURY
Atlântico Sul, 25 rua Professor Armando Ribeiro, tel:
(21) 2490-2050, e-mail:
reservas@atlanticosulhotel.
com.br A good way from
downtown on southern coast.

Santa Teresa
MID-RANGE
Santa Teresa Hotel, 660 rua
Almirante Alexandrino, tel:
(21) 2242-0007. In old-world
hilltop village. Bohemian
ambience. Go up by tramcar.

BUDGET
Bed and Breakfast Network,
Cama e Café, 67 rua Pro-
gresso, Santa Teresa, tel: (21)
2221-7653, e-mail: booking@
camaecafe.com.br
www.camaecafe.com.br Fifty
lovely family houses in Santa
Teresa. You can't go wrong.
Cama e Café Guest Card for
discounts in restaurants, bars,
stores and cultural centres.

São Conrado
LUXURY
Sheraton Rio, 121 av Nie-
meyer, tel: (21) 2274-1122.
Private beach. Outdoor envi-

Rio de Janeiro at a Glance

ronment, peaceful. Nice gym.
Intercontinental, 222 rua
Prefeto Mendes de Morais,
tel: (21) 2323-2200. Close to
green mountains and hang-
gliding area. Gym. Traditional
international restaurant.

YOUTH HOSTELS
Ipanema
Crab Hostel Brasil, 903
rua Prudente de Morais,
tel: (21) 2227-6130, e-mail:
ipanema@crabhostel.com.br
www.crabhostel.com.br

Copacabana
Shenkin Hostel, 304 rua
Santa Clara, tel: (21) 2257-
3133, e-mail: info@
shenkinhostel.com.br
www.shenkinhostel.com.br
Lockers, kitchen, bar, private
toilets. Breakfast is served
until late.
Che Lagarto Hostels, 87 rua
Anita Garibaldi, tel: (21) 2256-
2778, e-mail: copacabana@
chelagarto.com.br www.
chelagarto.com.br Non-stop
music, pool table, Internet.

Centro
**Association of Youth Hostels
of Rio de Janeiro**, 10/1.616
rua da Assembleía, tel: (21)
2531-2234, e-mail:
comercial@albergueda
juventude.com.br www.
alberguedajuventude.com.br

INN (POUSADA)
Pousada Katura Garden,
1245 estrada Barra de
Guaratiba, tel: (21) 2410-

1371, e-mail: atendimento@
katuragarden.com.br
www.katuragarden.com.br

APARTMENTS
Barra
Apart Hotéis, 1.120 av
Sernambetiba, Barra Beach,
tel: (21) 3389-6333. Combin-
ation of hotel and apartment.
There are dozens similar on
Barra da Tijuca promenade.

Copa and Ipanema, contact
Diamond David Diamante,
tel: (21) 2255-5355 (after
21:00), cell: 9626-3873,
e-mail: regency@openlink.
com.br

WHERE TO EAT

Quality of food, ambience
and service can put a small
inexpensive Rio restaurant
into top of the range.
Price ranges: R$40–70 and
above pp; R$20–40 pp; R$20
pp. US$1 = R$2.50 (2005
approx).
Azul Marinho, Hotel
Arpoador Inn, Av Francisco
Bhering, Arpoador, tel: (21)
3813-4228. Seats 68. Open
12:00–01:00 Mon–Thu,
12:00–02:00 Fri–Sat. R$50–
70. Amazing view and equally
amazing seafood. Seashore
ambience, Brazilian cuisine.
Moqueca do Gordinho, 1791
av Ayrton Senna, Barra da
Tijuca, tel: (21) 3325-7618,
seats 150 people. Open
12:00–00:00 Mon–Thu,
12:00–01:00 Fri–Sat, 10:00–
22:00 Sun. R$40–70. Fairly

pricey restaurant in a pricey
neighborhood. Specializes in
moqueca (a traditional dish
from Bahia – seafood served
with rice). Brazilian cuisine.
Salão Carioca, Hotel
Sheraton, 121 av Niemeyer,
Vidigal, tel: (21) 2529-1171.
Seats 250. Open 13:00–07:00
Sat. R$40–70. Serves tradi-
tional *feijoada* (black beans
and lots of meat), Saturday
buffet. Brazilian cuisine.
Filé de Ouro, 731 rua Jardim
Botânico, Jardim Botânico,
tel: (21) 2258-2396. Seats 40.
open 12:00–22:00 Mon–Sat;
R$40–70. The lines are huge
at the door, with people
wanting the house special,
which is a large lean fillet
steak. *A kilo*.
Marius, 290 av Atlântica,
Leme, tel: (21) 2543-6363.
Seats 210. Open 12:00–
16:00 and 18:00–00:00 Mon–
Fri, 12:00–00:00 Sat–Sun,
R$40–70. A variety of meats
that you won't find anywhere
else: frog, alligator, boar.
Royal Grill, store A, block G,
Casa Shopping, 2150 av
Ayrton Senna, Barra, tel: (21)
3325-6166. Seats 120. Open
daily, 12:00 until last diner
leaves. R$40–70. Á là carte.
Speciality dishes such as
arroz maluco (crazy rice).
Le Pré-Catelan, level E, Hotel
Sofitel Rio de Janeiro, 4240
av Atlântica, Copacabana, tel:
(21) 2525-1160. Seats 70.
Open 19:00–00:00 Mon–Sat.
Over R$70. Possibly the best
French cuisine in Rio. Atten-

tive service, mellow lighting, soft piano music.

Rêve D´Azur, 3 Ilha da Coroa, Barra, tel: (21) 2495-5880. Seats 52. Open 19:00–00:30 Sun–Mon. R$40–70. Romantic atmosphere. To get there, take a boat to the deck illuminated by torches. Tables lit by candlelight.

Natraj, 1219 av General San Martin, Leblon, tel: (21) 2239-4745. Seats 54. Open 19:00–00:00 Tue–Thu, 19:00–00:30 Fri–Sat, 12:30–23:00 Sun and holidays. R$40–70. They serve a good Indian *thali* (eight different dishes for two people, vegetarian and non-vegetarian).

Galani, 23 floor, Hotel Caesar Park, 460 av Vieira Souto, Ipanema, tel: (21) 2525-2535. Seats 80. Open 19:00–00:00 daily. Over R$70. Their Italian chef prepares some amazing dishes including a shrimp salad and great champignon sauce.

Cipriani, Hotel Copacabana Palace, 1702 av Atlântica, Copacabana, tel: (21) 2548-7070. Seats 50. Open 12:30–15:00 and 19:00–01:00 daily. Over R$70. Italian cuisine, and a great poolside view. Try the Palace's breakfast too.

Sushi Leblon, 256 rua Dias Ferreira, Leblon, tel: (21) 2512-7830 Seats 80. Open 19:00–01:30 Mon–Sat, 13:30–00:00 Sun. R$40–70. In the heart of Leblon. Very popular. Japanese.

Academia da Cachaça, 26-G rua Conde de Bernadote, Leblon, tel: (21) 2239-1542. Seats 80. Open 12:00–02:00 Tue–Sat, and 12:00–01:00 Sun–Mon. R$20–40. Tables across the sidewalk. Known for their 100 different types of *cachaça*. Northern Brazilian cuisine.

Acarajé das Estrelas, M-113, Barra Shopping, 4666 av das Américas, tel: (21) 2431-8162. Seats 44. Open 14:00–21:00 Mon, 10:00–21:00 Tue–Sat, 12:00–20:00 Sun. R$20–40. Dishes are named after famous Brazilian stars. Spicy Bahia food.

Balcão da Roça, stores 114–115, block 20, 500 av das Américas, downtown Barra, tel: (21) 2495-6686. Seats 140. Open 12:00–18:00 Sun–Thu, 12:00–02:00 Fri–Sat. R$20–40. Specializes in *mineira* cuisine from Minas Gerais province; over 60 different choices.

Bar do Arnaudo, 316-B rua Almirante Alexandrino, Santa Teresa, tel: (21) 2252-7246. Seats 60. Open 12:00–22:00 Tue–Fri, 12:00–20:00 Sat–Sun. R$20–40. The restaurant is over 32 years old and has always had a tradition of great food. Businessmen nip up here during their lunch break.

Bom Dia Maria, 10 rua Elvira Machado, Botafogo, tel: (21) 2275-6941. Seats 60. Open 12:00–18:00 Tue–Fri and

Sun, 19:00–00:00 Thu–Sat. R$20–40. This restaurant is over 100 years old and is known for incredible tropical foods from the Amazon, such as *açai* pizza and bread, turtle soup and spaghetti with shrimp sauce.

Casa da Feijoada, 10 rua Prudente Moraes, Ipanema, tel: (21) 2523-4994. Seats 62. Open 12:00–00:00 Mon–Sat, 12:00–23:00 Sun. R$20–40. Very rustic with carved wooden chairs and tables. The main plate is the *feijoada*, which comes with dessert and a drink included in the price.

Mala e Cuia, 123 av Presidente Wilson, Centro, tel: (21) 2524-5143. Seats 100. Open 11:00–16:00 Mon–Fri, 18:00–00:00 Thu–Fri. R$20–40. Tasty lunches, large portions. Lively atmosphere.

No Mar, Moqueca Capixaba, 782 av Maracanã, Tijuca, tel: (21) 2284-6843. Seats 80. Open 12:00–23:00 Tue–Fri, 12:00–00:00 Sat, 12:00–18:00 Sun. R$20–40. Try the *moqueca no mar* which has shrimp, squid, octopus and fish.

Três Potes, store 101, Barra Mall, 7700 av das Américas, tel: (21) 3326-2812. Seats 67. Open 12:00–00:00 Tue–Thu, 12:00–01:00 Fri–Sat, 12:00–22:00 Sun. R$20–40. *Mineira* cuisine. Their speciality is pork *filé*, which gives the meat a leaner taste.

Yemanjá, 128 rua Viscon de de Pirajá, Ipanema, tel:

Rio de Janeiro at a Glance

(21) 2247-7004. Seats 120. Open 18:00–00:00 Mon–Thu, 12:00–00:00 Fri–Sat, 12:00–22:00 Sun. R$20–40. Very creative seafood restaurant.

Yorubá, 94 rua Arnaldo Quintela, Botafogo, tel: (21) 2541-9387. Seats 48. Open 19:00–23:00 Wed–Fri, 14:00–22:00 Sat, 12:00–18:00 Sun. R$20–40. Amazing Afro-Bahia food. The establishment has been nominated several times as the best Brazilian restaurant in Rio.

El Patio Porteño, 1164 av Epitácio Pessoa, Lagoa, tel: (21) 2287-3947. Seats 120. Open 12:00–00:00 Mon–Thu, 12:00–01:00 Fri–Sat, 12:00–22:00 Sun. R$20–40. Everything is Argentinian, the owner, the meats and the way they cook them.

Estrela do Sul, Shopping Rio Off Price, 97 rua General Severiano, Botafogo, tel: (21) 2275-6280. Seats 350. Open 11:30–00:00 daily. R$20–40. They offer a great *rodizio* where the waiter brings different meats to the table and you choose from over 32 different cuts of meat, and a buffet with salads.

Grill 360º, 23 floor, Everest Rio Hotel, 1117 rua Prudente de Morais, Ipanema, tel: (21) 2525-2200. Open 12:00–15:30 and 19:00–00:00 daily. R$20–40. Awesome 360º view of Ipanema, the beach and the *lagoa*, is really what sells this eatery.

Majórica, 11 rua Senador Vergueiro, Flamengo, tel: (21) 2205-6820. Seats 250. Open 12:00–00:00 Mon–Thu and Sun, 12:00–01:00 Fri–Sat. R$20–40. Very traditional, and considered slightly upper class. Good meat, without the commotion of the *rodizios*.

Montana Grill, 777 av das Américas, Barra, tel: (21) 2491-4922. Seats 370. Open 12:00–00:00 Mon–Sat, 12:00–22:30 Sun. R$20–40. Run by a famous country-singing couple. Loved by celebrities.

Oásis, 136 estrada do Joá, São Conrado, tel: (21) 3322-3144. Seats 320. Open 11:00–00:00 daily, R$20–40. One of the finest *churrascaria* meat restaurants in Rio. There's even one dish cooked on granite that takes eight hours to prepare.

Afrodite Tis Milo, 288 rua Conde de Irajá, Botafogo, tel: (21) 2246-8430. Seats 120. Open 11:30–00:00 Sun–Thu, 11:30–02:00 Fri–Sat. R$20–40. Chef Anthony Ninos inherited his cooking abilities from his father. Mediterranean décor; traditional Greek dishes.

Adega Carne de Sol do Peixoto, 616 rua Barão de Mesquita, Tijuca, tel: (21) 2572-2296. Seats 200. Open 08:00–00:00 Tue–Sat, 08:00–18:00 Sun. R$20. Really good northern food in large portions.

Adega da Velha, 25 rua àulo

Barreto, Botafogo, tel: (21) 2286-2176, seats 70, open 07:00–01:00 daily, R$20. Tables spread out on the sidewalk.

À Mineira, 152 rua Visconde Silva, Humaitá, tel: (21) 2266-0520. Seats 240. Open 11:30–16:00 and 19:00–23:00 Mon–Wed, 19:00–00:00 Thu–Sat, 11:30–21:00 Sun. R$20. The food is made in wooden stoves; known for great price-value. Family favourite. Valet parking.

Arataca, store 4, Cobal do Leblon, Rua Gilberto Cardoso, Leblon, tel: (21) 2512-6249. Seats 28. Open 09:00–20:30 Tue–Thu, 10:00–21:00 Fri–Sat, 10:00–13:00 Sun. R$20. Since Tom Jobim, the famous Ipanema Girl composer, frequented this restaurant the clients have poured in.

Baixo Barra, store T, Shopping Esplanada da Barra, 3939 av das Américas, tel: (21) 2431-1760. Seats 80. Open from 12:00 until the last person leaves, Tue–Sun. R$20. Weight system; the best meat is 500g of *picanha*, a 'noble' meat.

Barra Brasa, store 125, Rosa Shopping, 120 av Marechal Henrique Lott, Barra, tel: (21) 3325-8653. Seats 120. Open 11:00–00:00 Sun–Mon. R$20. Located in Barra's gastronomic centre where people get together on fridays to have a *chopp* and *picanha*.

Rio de Janeiro at a Glance

A Grelha, 73 rua Garcia D´Ávila, Ipanema, tel: (21) 2239-6045 Seats 80. Open 12:00–00:00 daily. R$20. Most meat dishes are enough for two.

Author's Suggestions:
Confeitaria Colombo, 32 rua Gonçalves Dias, Centro, tel: (21) 2232-2300 (wise to make a luncheon reservation). Seats 200. Open Mon–Sat 08:00–20:00. R$70 plus. Supremely elegant 1894 Art-Nouveau restaurant and bar.
Eclipse, 1309 av NS de Copacobana, tel: (21) 2287-1788. Open daily until 03:00. R$10–20. Corner café-bar, excellent *chopp* and fast food. Hemingway characters argue football, *novellas*, politics and women.
Rio Sol e Mar, 11 av Repórter Nestor Moreira, Botafogo, tel: (21) 2543-1633. R$70. Very swish fish. Right on the water of Guanabara Bay. Sugar Loaf view.
Cafeína, 43 rua Farme de Amoedo, Ipanema, tel: (21) 2521-2194. Sidewalk café and bakery. Snacks and coffees. Watch Ipanema stroll by.

SHOPPING

Clothing: buy bikinis in Copa and Ipanema. Try Bumbum in the Fórum de Ipanema.
Books: for maps try Copa books Rua Francisco Sá, 26. Lj.A.Copacobana. Or Saraiva Mega Store, New York City

Center, Nível Térreo, Barra.
Jewellery: H. Stern and Amsterdam Sauer have fabulous selections of Brazil's many gemstones. Also free tours. Both are in Rua Garcia d'Ávila (113 and 105 respectively), Ipanema's high street. 'Diamond David' at Regency Gems and Jewelry is multilingual. 4240 av Atlântica, Copacabana.
Music: samba, bossa nova and everything in between, before and since, is available from many stores.
Bargains: Madureira Market is much cheaper than anywhere else. It is a wholesale shopping mall for street vendors and smaller retailers.
Food and drink: boxed figs, white cane rum or *cachaça* for making *caipirinhas*. There is even a tomato sauce called Goiachup made from guavas.
Traditional Crafts: try La Vereda in Santa Teresa or Pé de Boi in Laranjeiras.
Antiques: try Cassino Atlântico Mall near Sofitel Hotel in the southern corner of Copacabana Promenade.

TOURS AND EXCURSIONS

Experienced specialist tour-guide leaders include:
Paula Medeiros, tel: (21) 2225-6587, e-mail: paulainrio@hotmail.com and Raphael Shamoon Yuri Braga, e-mail: raphael_braga @hotmail.com
You can do a schooner tour around Guanabara Harbour,

a jeep tour in Tijuca National Park, a Sugar Loaf or City Tour, a tour up to Corcovado or attend a soccer match at Maracanã. For city and town tours, contact Louis Amaral, tel: (21) 2259-5532. For a jewellery manufacturing tour contact H. Stern, tel: (21) 2259-1011 (free hotel pick-up; free tour). Hang-gliding, tel: (21) 9343-3380. Helicopter tours, Helisight, tel: (21) 2511-2141. *Favela* tour, contact Marcelo Armstrong, tel: (21) 3322-2727 or (21) 9989-0074. Further afield, you can opt for the ten-hour suncoast tour to Búzios or Petrópolis in the mountains. Contact Petrópolis Italbus Turismo, tel: (21) 2589-6107. There are also historic Rio tours.

USEFUL CONTACTS

Federal Police, tel: (21) 2625-1530
Municipal Police, tel: 0800-211-532
Parks and Gardens, tel: (21) 2221-2574
Flight Information, tel: (21) 3398-4526
Bus Information, tel: (21) 2516-4802
Embassies/consulates:
South Africa, tel: (21) 2527-1455
UK, tel: (21) 2522-3123
Australia, tel: (21) 2518-3351
Argentina, tel: (21) 2551-0418
Israel, tel: (21) 2255-6940
Eire, tel: (21) 2281-4975
USA, tel: (21) 2292-7117.

Travel
Tips

Tourist Information
Rio Convention and Visitors Bureau, 547 rua Visconde de Pirajá, tel: (55-21) 2259-6165, e-mail: gerenciadeturismo@rcvb.com.br web: www. rioconventionbureau.co.br
Riotur, 9th floor, 10 rua Assembleía, Centro, tel: 0800-2000, tel: (55-21) 2542-8080, e-mail: riotur.riotur@pcrj.rj.gov.br web: www. riodejaneiro.turismo.com.br
Riotur Tourist Office: information kiosks at the main bus station (Rodoviária), the international airport, and an office in Copacabana at 183 av Princesa Isabel, tel: (55-21) 2541-7522.

Entry Requirements
Your passport must be valid for at least six months and you must have an onward or return ticket or proof that you can purchase one. Visas are not required by tourists from most countries for stays of up to 90 days. However US, Canadian, Australian and New Zealand passport holders require pre-entry visas obtainable for a fee from the nearest

Brazilian embassy, and not at a Brazilian port of entry. Visitors from, for example, African and Asian countries (except South Africa and Namibia) should check with their travel agent or nearest Brazilian Embassy. 90-day visas can only be renewed for another 90 days from the passport section of the federal Police at Praça Mauá in Centro (Av Venezuela). For business visas, check with nearest embassy.
Entry card: On arrival you'll be given a numbered entry card. By law you must keep a photocopy of this (and preferably a photocopy of your passport as well) on you at all times. The entry card must be returned to immigration when you leave. Lose it and you pay US$100.
Port Formalities: A yacht owner arriving in Rio should take all passports, visas and ship's papers to the following in this order: The Port Captain, Capitania dos Porto, tel: (21) 3870-5320, Federal Police, Customs (*Aduaneiras*), Health Authorities. Repeat the procession in reverse (except for Health) before leaving.

Customs: You can bring in new purchases to a value of US$500 duty free. Plus camera, video, laptop etcetera. Up to 24 alcoholic drinks. 400 cigarettes. 280g of perfume. You do not need to be warned by Customs. They will immediately spot you as a tourist and wave you through leaving the delicate decision to choose red or green to wicked Cariocas returning home with their foreign booty. (Passengers entering Brazil at São Paulo for transit to Rio collect luggage and clear customs at São Paulo, and re-check in).

Health Requirements
There are no special health requirements for entry into Rio unless you are coming from endemic disease areas (check with your travel agent). However, Yellow Fever is necessary if you are going on to visit Central-West of Brazil or Amazônia. Immunization against flu (aircraft are notorious), typhoid, polio, tetanus and hepatitis are a good idea if you're travelling around Brazil.

Getting There

See page 114.

What to Pack

Dress as if you are going to the tropics (Carioca man wears shorts, T-shirt and plastic slipslops. Carioca woman wears tight jeans, a short or sometimes a hip-hugging long skirt, top and designer slipslops). Always have a fold-up umbrella and in the 'winter' months (May–Aug), a rainproof jacket, long trousers and a jersey. Always have a hat. You would have to go to a very exclusive restaurant to need tie and jacket but wear long trousers in the evening. Some churches are wary of shorts. Swimming costume and a wraparound (*kanga*) are essential for the beach. Bring factor-30 suncream and shades. Swiss knife (in hold luggage) is always handy.

Money Matters

Currency: the Brazilian currency is the Real (R$) rather confusingly pronounced *hay-ow*; the plural Reais, *hay-ice*. It is split into 100 centavos with an extraordinary variety of coins. Notes come in 100, 50, 20, 10, 5 and 1 denominations. The 100 is unusual. Stick with a couple of 50s and R$200 in smalls when going out, including a few 50 centavo coins.
Exchange Rates: Brazil has gone through awful inflationary periods but by mid-2005 the currency had strengthened to ±US$1=R$2.30 (check on arrival). US dollars in cash are much more negotiable than

any other currency. Keep a few on you plus a credit card. Hotels give a lower (about 15%) exchange rate than banks. Not all banks exchange forex (HSBC, Citibank, Banco do Brasil are three of the best). Check, for example, *O Globo* newspaper for the daily rate. Travel cheques are not advisable as you can pay a hefty premium for changing them. Rather keep your US$ forex cash in your hotel room safe.
Credit Cards and ATMs are widely used and the best thing to carry. Visa is best. Be careful when using your card: watch the operators; do not let your waiter take it away. Some ATMs (*see* above banks) will ask you if you want your transaction in English. There is no black market. There are plenty of *câmbios* or money-change shops. Keep your lost credit card telephone number of your home country on you.

Accommodation

Reserve accommodation (ideally on the web) well before you leave and particularly just before if you are visiting Rio during, and after Carnaval, and in the July school holidays. Copacabana and Ipanema are probably the most convenient places public transport-wise, and if you're sea-facing, the most beautiful. Less expensive accommodation is available off-promenade but has more traffic noise. Off-season do not hesitate to ask for a discount over the 'rack' rate that hotels

worldwide initially quote, whether you book in advance or when you arrive. All Rio receptionists are prepared to deal. You will get a polite and faintly amused refusal in high season. Breakfast is usually included in the price. (*See* also Where to Stay, page 114).

Eating Out

Eating out is the Rio thing. Only eat in your hotel if you're exhausted when you arrive. There are a thousand restaurants in Rio, let alone hundreds of corner *chopp* bar-eateries, cafés, takeaways, beachside kiosks and *sucos* fruit-juice outlets. They range from tiny holes-in-the-wall with two pavement tables to 'noble' restaurants with 100 tables. Then there are the famous Rio *botequims*, (about 60 of them) – old family-run bars and restaurants with superb food and home-made beer. You must try an *a-kilo* restaurant. Help yourself to salads and choose cuts of meat from the fire – you are charged what it weighs. Some restaurants on Copacabana have dozens of tables on the pavement promenade beneath the trees, Paris-style. A little touristy. For two persons: budget less than R$30; mid-range R$60; luxury R$100. Wine is extra and tends to be expensive in spite of the fact that reasonable wines are produced in Brazil. Tipping 10%. (Taxis don't expect it but appreciate it.)

Transport
See Getting There and Getting Around, page 114.

Business Hours
09:00–18:00 Mon–Fri (shops until 19:00); 09:00–13:00 Sat (including post offices). The big American-style shopping malls are usually open 10:00–22:00 daily. Banks are open 10:00–16:00 Mon–Fri. Restaurants stay open late.

Time
Rio time is GMT minus three. In effect, five hours behind Johannesburg and 14 hours behind Sydney. Daylight-saving time is Oct–Feb/May (clocks go an hour forward).

Communications
Telephones: the international dialing code for Rio is: 55 21 followed by the appropriate eight-digit number. As there are a variety of private telephone companies in Brazil, to phone abroad start with 00 then either 14, 15, 21, 23 or 31, followed by your country code, city code and number. (21 is the usual one of these five) When making national calls dial 21 followed by the eight digit local number. Rio's blue hideaway call boxes are everywhere and known as Big Brother Ears or *orelhões*. You can buy phone cards from post offices and telephone offices. Magazine kiosks also sell them.

Mobiles: known as a handy or cellular in Rio. Check with your mobile service provider before leaving home to see if your package will function in Rio. Brazil has a GS 1800 network among others. You can rent a cellular from many places. PressCell for example, tel: (21) 3322-2692 or 9617-2000, will deliver to your hotel.

Internet cafés: There are plenty of internet (and telephone) cafés. Try **Locutório**, loja B, 26 rua Franciso Sá, tel: (21) 2522-6343 or **Cyber Phone**, loja D, 99 Praça Demétrio Ribeiro, tel: (21) 2295-3333, both in Copacabana. Prices can be as low as R$3.50 an hour.

Faxes: in most *correios* (post offices) and some hotels.

Post: allow one, maximum two weeks for postcards to arrive. Postage is quite expensive.

Electricity
Carry an adapter. Check the voltage. The current is 110 or 120 volts, 60 cycles, AC. Most power points have sockets for both round and flat prongs.

Weights and Measures
Brazil uses the metric system.

Health Precautions
Most people drink water in blue bottles but the tap water is safe (except outside Rio). Treat travel **diarrhoea** with 500mg of Ciprofloxacin (you can buy it across the counter), every 12 hours. Drink a lot of water or diluted cola. Do not eat meat cooked at pavement

	CONVERSION CHART	
FROM	**TO**	**MULTIPLY BY**
Millimetres	Inches	0.0394
Metres	Yards	1.0936
Metres	Feet	3.281
Kilometres	Miles	0.6214
Square kilometres	Square miles	0.386
Hectares	Acres	2.471
Litres	Pints	1.760
Kilograms	Pounds	2.205
Tonnes	Tons	0.984
To convert Celsius to Fahrenheit: x 9 ÷ 5 + 32		

barbecue's. There is usually no **malaria** in the city but occasionally its comrade-in-arm, **dengue**, makes an appearance. Beware of **HIV – AIDS**. A whole range of nasties are out there in the jungle and remote country areas including **rabies**, **snake-bite**, **ticks**, **bilharzia**, and **sunburn** that causes skin cancer. Take out **medical travel insurance** before leaving. Private medical and dental services are excellent in Rio (check with your consulate as to English-speaking physicians). You will normally need a prescription for drugs but if you know what you want, try a couple of chemists first. Go with a Portuguese speaker. Always be wary of blood transfusions anywhere in the world. Make sure any needle is opened in front of you. Be a little wary of doctors and travel guides in your home country that advise you to have 101 pre-travel inoculations. **Medical Advisory Service to Travellers Abroad** (web: www.masta.org) and the **NHS** in the UK (web: www.fitfortravel.scot.nhs.uk) both offer useful information.

Medical Emergencies

Medical Rescue, Amil, tel: (21) 2533-1000 and **Golden Cross**, tel: (21) 2533-1000. **Ambulance**, tel: 193. **Alcoholics Anonymous**, tel: (21) 2253-9283. **AIDS Centre**, tel: (21) 2518-2221. **Blood Bank**, tel: (21) 2242-6080. **Galdino Campos Cárdia Copa** (English-speaking 24-hour clinic) Av NS de Copacabana, tel: (21) 2548-9966.

Personal Safety

With a third of Rio's population being poor, petty theft such as bag-snatching is the city's main drawback. However, the popular visitor areas such as Copacabana are well policed, specifically to avoid this. Wearing a money belt pouch immediately identifies you as a gringo (foreigner). Don't be too flash with jewellery and cameras. Photocopy your passport, airticket and entry card and carry them with you. Do not leave valuables in hotel rooms – use the hotel safe. Never go into *favelas* unless accompanied by someone who is accepted by the community or is streetwise or is a local NGO, or you are on a conducted tour. The City Centre tends to be deserted at night and on Sundays. Walk around on Sundays but preferably not on your own. (Watch out for slippery black and white mosaic sidewalks, especially when its raining.) Under no circumstances bring narcotics into Rio. They are not legal, the penalties are high and there are lots of cops. If threatened with theft or violence, hand over your goodies politely or bargain if you speak Portuguese. Anyone in a rather rugged boots-'n-badges uniform is usually one of the several police forces in Rio: Federal (traffic), Police Militar (normal street police), Guarda Municipal and in places like Copacabana and the Central Bus Station, Tourist Police.

Road Signs

The usual international road signs are used in Rio. As a pedestrian be careful at traffic lights which can vary. The 'do not cross' light can be red or yellow, often a hand signifying 'halt'. Do not jaywalk like everybody else until you have been in Rio a few days. Rio is pro-car rather than pro-pedestrian. And traffic is speedy and competitive.

Emergencies

Police, tel: 190.
Tourist Police, tel: (21) 3399-7170 and 2511-5112.
Fire, tel: 193.
Ambulance, tel: 193.

Etiquette

Cariocas do not mind how you dress. Just be sensible if you are going out at night, going into a government office or into a church. Cariocas are multiracial, multicultural, decent, and kind people. Any form of bad temper or aggressive body language would be quite shocking to them. Trying to speak a little Portuguese works wonders.

Language

Cariocas do not speak a lot of English, although those in the tourism and hotel business are often fluent in several European languages. Use a phrase book, speak slowly and practice your sign language. Someone will usually offer to help translate and practice his/her English. Spanish, Italian, German are all useful.

Special Interest Groups

Disabled travellers: With a few exceptions, there are few sidewalk wheelchair ramps in Rio. The special **City Rio** tourist bus service runs every 30 minutes, running the length of the city. Tickets can be purchased at the larger hotels or on the buses. These buses are disabled-friendly.
Children: Cariocas love children and will usually go out of their way to help family groups.
Student travellers: An International Student Identity Card (ISIC) including photo issued by travel agencies in your home country will sometimes get you special discounted prices at hotels, cinemas and on transport.
Gay and lesbian travellers: We often feel threatened by the unusual or the unknown.

Not so in Rio; Cariocas are completely relaxed about sexuality in any form. Some of the very best, and most entertaining Carnaval samba groups are gay. There is no law against homosexuality in Brazil (web: www. riogayguide.com)
Single women: Take the usual precautions about not going out at night on your own to lonely places, for example, the beach. Be prepared to be chatted up; its part of Carioca-man's charisma and par for the course.
Senior Travellers: There is excellent inter-age rapport in Rio where, no matter how old you are, you are not perceived as being 'over the hill'. You are merely in the 'third age' (*tercio idade*) or, to use the affectionate expression used by the locals, 'ripe'.

GOOD READING

- **Ângelo, Ivan** (1992) *Benjamin*, Bloomsbury. Novel set during the military dictatorship.
- **Danusia, Barbara** (2004) *Guide to Rio Restaurants*, Senac Rio. Very detailed. English-Portuguese.
- **Drummond de Andrade Carlos** (1986) *Travelling in the Family: Selected Poems*, Random House. Brazil's greatest poet.
- **Goslin, Priscilla Ann** (2000) *How to be a Carioca – The Alternative Guide for the Tourist in Rio*. Amusing.
- **Guia Rádio Rock, Guia Quatro Rodas**. Yearly guide to all surfing, swimming, diving and fishing spots around Rio and São Paulo. Portuguese. Good maps.
- **Lispector, Clarice** (1986) *The Hour of the Star*, Manchester: Carcanet. Brazil's top woman writer.
- **Nogueira, Cristiano** (2004) *Rio for Partiers*, Solcat Publishing. Irreverent guide for music lovers and party animals. English.
- **Rio Prefeitura Municipality** (among others) (2004) *Rio Botequim*, Casa da Palavra. Old Rio bars/restaurants. Portuguese.
- **Rio Prefeitura Riotur**, *Monthly Guide to Rio*, City of Rio de Janeiro Tourism Authority. Events, sights, museums, everything.

INDEX

Note: Numbers in **bold** indicate photographs